THE HYMNODY OF THE CHRISTIAN CHURCH

THE LECTURES
ON "THE L. P. STONE FOUNDATION"
PRINCETON THEOLOGICAL SEMINARY
1926

BY
LOUIS F. BENSON, D.D.

NEW YORK
GEORGE H. DORAN COMPANY

THE HYMNODY OF THE CHRISTIAN CHURCH
— B —
PRINTED IN THE UNITED STATES OF AMERICA

PREFACE

A good Providence has committed to the hands of every pastor, for such use as he can make of them, the three arts that lie nearest the human heart,—speech, poetry and music. The mission of poetry and music no doubt transcends the limits of congregational singing, but nevertheless it proves most spiritually effective in a self-expression by the people themselves in common song.

With these thoughts in mind I welcomed the call to deliver the Stone Lectures at Princeton as an opportunity to present the whole subject of our Christian Hymnody to those soon to be concerned in its administration in a way that might prove helpful in preparing them for so great a responsibility. In retaining the lecture-form here I have sought not only to express my appreciation of the original opportunity but also to retain something of the larger freedom of direct address.

In preparing the lectures for print I have omitted most of the passing pleasantries (and other things) that emphasized the ecclesiastical connection of the lecturer and a majority of his hearers. But even in a book for wider use, if that may be, it is convenient to have our thoughts directed to some specific object, whether it be a focusing point for one's rambling reflections or a target for one's reproaches. And so, amid references to many communions, I have here and there singled out the Presbyterian to serve such a purpose; particularly in making, for reasons fully stated, its *Hymnal* of 1895 the basis for a discussion of the textual criticism of hymns.

The motive that runs through the book like a recurrent refrain is that the hymn belongs among the things of the spirit, and that hymnody is essentially a spiritual function. The hymn is a melody in the individual heart: hymnody is the harmony of brotherhood.

Lecture I reveals its spiritual foundation. Lecture II shows how precariously, even in the Church, the hymn, like other things of the spirit, has maintained a footing. Lecture III shows how the elusive, spiritual thing we call a hymn relates itself to the forms of speech we call literature. Lectures IV and V take up the religious functions of the hymn, its spiritual and literary content, its fit expression. The last lecture discusses the spiritualization of music, to the end that the hymn may fulfill its destiny as common song.

Hymnody, then, is a spiritual function, and its welfare proceeds from the heart. Nevertheless its congregational expression needs guidance and a thoughtful ordering as much now as at Corinth in the days of St. Paul. Most of all it needs the inspiration which can only be imparted to preoccupied hearts by a pastor who cherishes it as among the best of God's gifts, and understands it because he has learned the lessons of its chequered history, has measured its resources and traced the different lines of its ministry; and who is resolute to cultivate the spirit of song among his people.

It is the special purpose of this book to furnish the materials for that better understanding of Christian Hymnody as a preparation for getting the most we can out of it in life and worship.

Beyond expressing a sense of the practical importance of the subject I do not know that I can offer any inducement to read the book except to say that I have made it as interesting as I could. I might add that it takes the place of a Primer of Hymnology long in mind, and that even its dullest passages press more lightly upon human patience than the primer would have done.

Philadelphia,
July 27th, 1927.

CONTENTS

LECTURE ONE

THE APOSTOLIC IDEAL OF HYMNODY

LECTURE TWO

THE RELATION OF THE HYMN TO HOLY SCRIPTURE

LECTURE THREE

THE RELATION OF THE HYMN TO LITERATURE

LECTURE FOUR

THE CONTENTS OF THE HYMN

LECTURE FIVE

THE TEXT OF THE HYMNS

LECTURE SIX

HYMN SINGING

LECTURE ONE

THE APOSTOLIC IDEAL OF HYMNODY

LECTURE ONE

THE APOSTOLIC IDEAL OF HYMNODY

I begin with a simple expression of satisfaction; not so much that the reverend Faculty have again recognized Hymnology as a subject worthy of a hearing, as that they have once more made a place for it in a lectureship confined by its founder to "topics kindred to theological studies." They confirm its title to a place in the crowded ranks of theological disciplines that make for the preparation of the ministry of the gospel.

To this word of appreciation I should like to add a few more in regard to the study of Hymnology itself and to the marks of that kinship with theological studies.

There is to-day no complaint more general from those who still care for the services of God's House than that against the way in which the interests of the people are disregarded in the administration of church song. In liturgical Churches the complaint is that the participation of the congregation is becoming more difficult and often impracticable. In "non-liturgical" Churches the complaint is that the pastors treat congregational song as perfunctory and negligible; to be disposed of by following the lines of least resistance; or else that they use it in a way that makes it simply a reënforcement or extension of the voice of the preacher rather than an opportunity for the people to express the things God puts into their hearts. And who could withhold some sympathy from these long-suffering complainants?

Naturally their criticisms go beyond the pastor to the theological school that turned him out. They express a conviction that however he may have been equipped for the ministry of the Word, he was not properly trained to administer the Hymnody. My own opinion is that in this matter (and the present occasion confirms it) our seminaries are feeling their way. There are at all events some things to be suggested looking toward a suspension of judgment.

We all know what a problem the curriculum of a theological school has become, and the multitude of studies clamoring for recognition. Hymnology is one of the latest of these claimants, and weakened its claim by starting among ourselves on a wrong turn.

Hymnology was made in Germany, the fatherland of the modern hymn. English-speaking Protestantism turned its back on Lutheran songs. It reverted to the inspired Psalm as the only authorized "subject-matter of praise." And the correlated study was Exegetics. When the singing of "human composures" had become familiar, "Hymnology" meant simply the body of hymns collectively. I cannot satisfy myself that the word was used in its proper sense of the study of them until the nineteenth century was growing old. Lord Selborne's famous article, "Hymns," in the *Encyclopædia Britannica* of 1881 fought shy of it. Dr. Julian's *Dictionary of Hymnology* (1892) first made the name familiar and first covered the subject.

An interest in hymns had awakened before that. But it was disposed to treat them as "Sacred Poetry," as a minor department of English literature, which, when not conspicuous for charm, was retrieved by moral values. It was a wrong start; not so much because of the pious assumption that the hymn was to be included within the domain of poetry as because any dealings with it as "mere literature" dissevered it from its motive, its environment and its function; thus making it a sort of literary bric-a-brac. That accounts for the nervous irritation, not to say the spirit of derision, in which our hymns have been ever since regarded by literary critics. Perhaps it may make the more modest claim of the newer Hymnology to a kinship with theological studies seem less of a venture than a counsel of prudence.

I. The Hymn

1. *In Its Relation to Theology*

The kinship of these studies becomes more discernable and more suggestive if we trace it along the tripled lines on which our hymns exercise their religious functions.

(a) *They are a singularly effective medium of Christian doctrine,*—as a container of doctrine and as a circulating medium, but, back of all that, as a means to the spiritual apprehension of truth and its expression devotionally.

The theologian and the hymn writer traverse day by day the same country, the Kingdom of our Lord. They walk the same paths; they see the same objects; but in their methods of observation and their reports of what they see they differ. So far as Theology is a science the theologian deals simply with the topography of the country: he explores, he measures, he expounds. So far as hymn writing is an art the writer deals not with the topography but with the landscape: he sees, he feels, and he sings. The difference in method is made inevitable by the variance of temperament of the two men, the diversity of gifts. But both methods are as valid as inevitable. Neither man is sufficient in himself either as an observer or a reporter. It is the topography and the landscape together that make the country what it is. It is didactics and poetry together that can approach the reality of the spiritual kingdom.

Poetry is always an illumination, and sometimes an actual discovery, of truth through imagination and feeling. And for mystical aspects of truth poetry and music afford the only available expression. We all feel that with some Scripture Psalms and some great hymns we take in more truth than we could shape didactically. Maybe it is only light and color, but it *is* illumination. He would be a dry-as-dust theologian who shrank from using Psalm or hymn in explication of his themes. It is more important to remember that in the mind of the plain everyday Christian, where feeling conditions reflection so strongly, the hymns he uses devotionally, and especially those he loves, do more to form his religious thinking than anything else except the Bible.

For doctrine, then, the hymn book takes its place beside the catechism. And Hymnology thus supplements Catechetics.

(b) *Hymns are equally effective as helps toward Christian living.*

To bring the inspirations of poetry to bear upon the religious life is the Church's unending task. The most natural solution is to provide a collection of lyrics of life and duty, and to keep it fresh and appealing by revisions as circumstance and feeling change. This the Jewish Church did in her Psalter, and this most of the Christian communions try to do, whether by modernizing that Psalter or by providing hymns of their own. That is to say the Church puts in her people's hands two books: the canon of Scripture as the revelation of the spiritual view of life, and a canon of hymnody as a manual of the spiritual life.

The hymnal thus ranks as "a means of grace,"

and Hymnology becomes "kindred to theological studies." The content of the two canons must accord. The searchlights of Christian Ethic must play upon the hymnody. Poetic sentiment must submit to the restraints of a sound Christian Psychology.

(c) *Hymns are the most effective medium for the people's participation in public worship.*

And when their singing becomes a recognized part of worship Hymnology becomes a branch of Liturgics.

Liturgics is the study of the philosophy, the history and administration of public worship. The chairs in many theological schools seem to have been named in a spirit of excluding Liturgics from Reformed Theology. If so the protest was quite vain. Theology deals with the knowledge of God: Liturgics is the application of that knowledge to His worship. "God is a spirit" is theology. "They that worship Him must worship in spirit and in truth" is liturgics,—the heart of it. This division of Churches into "liturgical" and "non-liturgical" is easily misapprehended. There is no such thing as a non-liturgical Church other than one in which a prescribed formula of worship is not imposed by authority. I always feel at Friends' Meeting that the very restraints constitute a form of worship, and that the unwritten rubrics are distinctly liturgical.

Zwingli, as we all know, tried to persuade the Reformed Church that preaching and hearing sermons was the only worship. In our own communion at least all such misapprehensions and even the later Puritan exaltation of preaching over worship are repudiated in the Church constitution, which declares:

"As one primary design of public ordinances is to pay social acts of homage to the most high God, ministers ought to be careful not to make their sermons so long as to interfere with or exclude the more important duties of prayer and praise" (*Directory for Worship*, VII, vii).

Church song finds place here among the acts of social homage more important than sermons rather than as an appendage to them. Hymnology therefore relates itself to Theology through Liturgics and not Homiletics.

The distinction is important in two directions. First, in its compelling insistence upon bringing the church hymnal four square to the church constitution. It seems obvious that any communion which discards the homiletical ideal of worship is bound to provide its congregations with a hymnal that shall be a service-book rather than a cyclopedia of religious verse coördinated by an "Index of Scripture texts."

The distinction bears also upon theological education. It suggests that the training in Hymnology already referred to should be along the lines of a preparation for the liturgical use of church hymnody, apart from sermon illustration. It is no doubt a line that to many an eager heart, thrilled by the call to preach the gospel, will seem to be a theological discipline in the most onerous sense.

2. *In Comparative Religion*

It is quite time to put the question—What is a hymn? If you looked it up in *Webster*, the *Century*, the *Standard*, and in the disappointingly meager offering of the great *Oxford Dictionary*, you would, I think, find it puzzling to strike a common denominator. Most of us by now are accustomed to regard as hymns the songs to Pagan divinities used in ritual. But hymnody has had recently a new development by the band of scholars coöperating in *The Dictionary of Religion and Ethics* under Dr. Hastings' undaunted lead. The opening article of its seventh volume gathers into 116 columns, under the compendious title of "Hymns," the best account in English of what we used to call "The sacred poetry of early religions,"[1]—Babylonian, Vedic, Egyptian, Greek, Celtic, etc., as well as Jewish and Christian. But, says one of the writers, we shall have to extend our "use of the word 'hymn' to include some more or less philosophical poems" and also the versified spells or charms against hostile powers used on the lower or magical side of religion.

Whether this extension brings gain or confusion will be decided differently. Most likely the label so affixed in an influential quarter will stick. And there are enough materials gathered there to indicate a new study—Comparative Hymnology. We shall have to revise our nomenclature accordingly and accept the designation of "Christian Hymnology" for what concerns us here and now. *Christian Hymnology* was indeed the precise title given in 1870 by Dean Murray of Princeton to his little book on hymns. But by "Christian" he meant only to mark them off from Jewish Psalms, and by "Hymnology" he no doubt meant Hymnody.

3. *In Its Christian Definition*

What is the Christian hymn, of which we speak so familiarly; and manage to get ourselves understood, after a fashion?

In the Septuagint "humnos" applies to Psalms voicing Israel's praise. But in the New Testament St. Paul twice refers to "hymns" in a way to distinguish them from Psalms—"Psalms *and* hymns." St. Augustine,[2] who was captivated by the new metrical strains of Ambrose, limits the word to "songs with praise to God." "Without praise," he claims, "they are not hymns," and "if they praise aught beside God," they are not.

Augustine's became the recognized church definition. But is it not a bit dogmatic? Are all the Psalms pure praise? And from Homer and Hesiod down "humnos" had applied to songs or odes addressed to other gods and to heroes. Our English poets by common consent have followed the classical and not the church tradition; from Spenser's earlier "Hymne in honour of Love" to Shelley's "Hymn to Intellectual Beauty" and Swinburne's "Hymn to Proserpina." Even our irreproachable Longfellow has his "Hymn to the Night."

Even modern Christian practice itself shows no agreement as to what makes a hymn.

When we speak of the hymns of the Greek Church, most of us have in mind the metrical versions Neale and Brownlie have prepared for congregational use. But the originals are in prose, not verse. They are set into the texts of the various offices, often so interlaced with Psalm or gospel or homily that only an expert can unravel the tangle. And they are not sung by the congregation or put into their hands, but reserved for the officiants alone.

In the Roman Catholic Church, "Hymns" are the versified devotions inserted in the prose Psalms of the Daily Office, as distinguished from the "Sequences" of the Mass. They are not vernacular but Latin. They are not sung by the people, and outside of monasteries it is enough that the priests read them in silence. Nowadays that communion has also its own popular hymns for certain uses and occasions.

In the Anglican Church the makers of the Prayer Book called the prose "Te Deum" and "Benedictus" hymns, but not so the L. M. and C. M. versions of "Veni Creator." The editors of successive editions seem on the whole to have thought of a hymn as a prose canticle taken from the New Testament in contrast with an Old Testament Psalm.

In early American Presbyterianism "hymn" was a term of adventure or reproach. It covered verses of human manufacture offered to take the place of inspired Psalms. To our separated Presbyterian brethren that meaning and that reproach still linger in the word.

In fact all these varied applications still linger in the word. And if we are to discuss hymns rationally we must remember them all. The only feature common throughout seems to be the intent of use in worship. A Christian hymn therefore is a form of words appropriate to be sung or chanted in public devotions. Almost every Protestant hymn book contains the prose "Te Deum," ill-adapted as it is to congregational singing, and some prose Psalms and canticles set to chants. At the same time an immense preponderance of metrical compositions, divided into stanzas that a congregation can sing by repeating the tune to each one, shows that such in the main is the present-day Protestant conception of the word "hymn."

And that is perhaps all we can do in the way of defining the word in our Christian usage.

II. The Inauguration of Christian Song

In the studies of Christian Hymnody we are now to make, what I have really at heart are its present-day interests rather than those of antiquarianism. None the less we shall have to proceed by the historical method,—a length-wise approach by the way things happened rather than a cross-country sketch of the way things are. Such is the common lot of all students of human institutions. For man is an old resident, and all that he is and has is mediated through the past.

In the study of a church ordinance the historical method is imperative. We must first seek its roots in New Testament times and trace its continuity through church history before we can frame a working theory for its proper administration.

Here and now, for example. Is there a Christian ordinance which we may call Holy Song, with Christ's authority behind it? And if so, on what terms did the Apostolic Church receive it and practice it? What features were present from the beginning, and must therefore be regarded as essential to its being? And, among the features of its later church practice, which are to be regarded as developments contributing to its well-being and which as mere accretions and perhaps hindrances? When we have answered these questions, and only so, it seems to me, we have our working theory of church song.

The contribution which even a superficial study of Comparative Hymnology makes to the study of origins is in relieving us of any necessity to discuss a theoretical relation of music and religion. It shows us that relation as already a condition and not a theory in early religions. It reveals the actual employ of hymns in ritual and life from a time earlier than all written records. It shows especially a relatively high development of worship-music and poetry in one of those national religions, the Hebrew, and how in the divine providence that Jewish Psalmody became the inheritance of the Christian Church, passing into it directly and unquestioned.

The actual point of transition is found at the institution of the Lord's Supper. The simple record in its Englished form, "And when they had sung an hymn, they went out into the Mount of Olives," has always touched the Christian heart. For our present occasion its significance lies in revealing Christ as Himself the inaugurator of our church song and in His connecting it with the most characteristic feature of Christian worship—the Holy Communion.

This post-Communion hymn was ritual song, and must have been so sensed by the disciples. Thus it became at once not only the precedent but the spring of our church song, which in all the main streams that have started from it continues to be ritual song. But (the occasion being what it was) the precedent is just as valid, if one were needed, for the social simplicities of hymnody, the worship-song of a household, the friendly song of a brotherhood.

If we ask the manner of singing at the Supper, it was common song in the sense that all joined in, but antiphonal, or more likely responsive, in actual delivery. Would the disciples wait for the Master to begin? Or was there some one with special aptness to start the song?

If we put the question of our Western poet, "What song sang the twelve with the Saviour?"—the rapt and isolated song of spiritual possession was so soon to interrupt the common song, that I suppose the thought has come to most of us that in the stress of the occasion the parting song might have been an inspirational hymn of the Master, with some familiar response by the disciples. Such a thought came certainly to the author of the *Acta Johannis*, who pictures the little group standing hand in hand, and even gives the words of the hymn.[8] He may have crystallized some rumor or tradition, or may have drawn at first hand upon a seemingly ample reserve of mendacity.

The record does not identify the hymn and the verb used does not point in any particular direction. It is a part of the case of our brethren who would for all time confine church praise to Old Testament Psalms that our Lord gave out one of them, establishing a precedent and implying a prescription. If so the Evangelists seem to have been very much at fault not to have told us.

And yet the company must have sung something familiar, and what so familiar as the Psalms? And as the Master began by adhering to the Passover ritual, what so natural as to conclude with the second part of the Hallel, appointed as a thanksgiving for the fourth cup? Most scholars agree that He did so.[4] Professor Bickell, who thinks the Hallel was concluded before the Communion, argues for the fresh selection of some appropriate Psalm, the 23rd preferably:[5] a suggestion that at all events makes a sentimental appeal.

The Presbyterian Communion service, when properly set and administered, is unique in being a dramatic portrayal of the original occasion. Such was its intent, and so much of the record is quoted as to make it surprising that the post-Communion hymn was not dealt with more suggestively. Knox's *Book of Common Order* provided that "the action being ended, the people sing the 103rd Psalm, or some other of thanksgiving"; but the Westminster *Directory for Worship* omitted this rubric altogether. Our American Directory, however, provides, a bit casually: "Now let a psalm or hymn be sung, and the congregation dismissed."

III. Christian Song in the Jewish-Christian Church

Both precedents, the feast and the Psalm, were followed by the brethren at Jerusalem; who "breaking bread from house to house, did eat their meat with gladness and singleness of heart, praising God" (Acts ii, 46, 47). They had been accustomed to use the Psalms devotionally all their lives, and under the new circumstances would continue to use them with quickened feelings. St. Peter's sermon shows how the Master had trained them to read new meanings into the hallowed words.

These first Christians are described as in that state of spiritual elation out of which song springs as naturally as flowers blossom. And plainly they felt perfectly free to add new songs to the old, which the more gifted among them did from the beginning.

St. Luke gathers up three of these Jewish-Christian Psalms into his gospel of the Infancy, the "Magnificat," the "Benedictus," and the "Nunc Dimittis." So Jewish that, as Dr. Warfield said,[6] to have met the Magnificat in the midst of the Psalter would have occasioned no suspicion: so Christian that they still form a part of the daily office of the Church. In view of which fact Dean Farrar has ventured to confer upon the anthologist the fanciful title of "the first hymnologist."[7]

Where did St. Luke get these lyrics? The suggestion that he found them in the Church's hymn book has nothing against it except a lack of evidence of any such employment before the fifth century. On the other hand the suggestion that Jewish Christians did not feel as free to sing as to make such new songs is against the probabilities of the situation. It is an intrusion of presumptions to support a theory that the Church inherited the Psalter as a sealed hymn book under a perpetual Act of Uniformity.

To most students that early atmosphere seems to embody a spirituality of the creative sort, of expansion rather than compulsory restriction. It appears to have been a divine providence rather than a divine prescription that laid the Psalter ready to the Church's hand, and as though its contents rather than the urgency of its rubrics recommended its use to the first Christians.

The only example of a Jewish-Christian Psalm in actual employ is in Acts iv, where the company "lift up their voice to God with one accord" in words beginning "O Lord, Thou art God, which hast made heaven and earth, and the sea." It shows a freedom in dealing with ancient formularies of prayer and praise.

The group in St. Luke more fully illustrates the earliest stage of the new Psalm making. Its structure closely following the Psalter model; its substance reminiscent of Psalm and prophecy; its criterion the clear note of Messianic fulfillment. It was a gospel appendix to the Davidic Psalter.

The thing most characteristic of this primitive Christian song, so memorable as to color the record, is the gladness of the singers' hearts, the predominance of praise. It was natural that both of our poets who celebrated the hymn at the Last Supper, emphasized its pathos. It was "a mournful song," John Pierpont says;

> "And sad, I should say, as the winds are,
> That blow by the white gravestones."

adds Joaquin Miller. If this were so it is important to remember that the sadness belonged to the human as distinguished from the spiritual side of Christian song as there inaugurated. Nor was it in the words sung. It came from the foreshadow of the Master's impending absence on human hearts, their failure of faith to foresee His abiding presence. And when they came more fully under the influence of His Spirit their song lost forever its human plaintiveness and bubbled over with joy and gladness, with "praising God" first of all and with the happiness of fellowship in and with Christ.

I infer, then, that this note of gladness is the special offering of Jewish-Christian song toward our theory of hymnody, whether as an essential thing necessary to its being or as a characteristic thing necessary to its well-being. I infer that our own hymns, in so far as they are fully spiritual, are cheerful and not sad, "joyful in the Lord"; that the plaintive and sobbing verse, the complaints and anxieties in which our hymnals are so rich, and most of all the obsession of so many of our songs with the foreshadowing of death, are not in reality nearly so spiritual as we have supposed them to be. They are voices of questionings and doubts that come from the outward show of things and the lack of health within combining to obscure from the singers' eyes the reality and joy of the perpetual Presence.

IV. Christian Song in the Gentile Churches

1. *The Liberty of Christian Praise*

So far as we can picture the development of Christian song in the churches St. Paul founded, it was at first a rivulet flowing in the old channels of Jewish psalmody; then swelling into a flood that for a while leaped the banks and hid the original stream, through the outpouring of heavenly gifts of inspirational song; which, subsiding, left an enriched but perhaps unquiet stream to flow in the steady course of a recognized church ordinance.

The Jews scattered through the Empire served as a nucleus for mission churches. The general familiarity with "common Greek," and the circulation of the Septuagint with its Psalter, and of any Jewish-Christian Psalms that were available, furnished an equipment for common praise of the familiar sort.

So much is obvious. But it omits the Gentile converts. However loyally they received the Psalter from the hands of their Jewish brethren, can we doubt that their incoming inevitably led to what the Scots used to call "Some enlargement of the Psalmody." Allow for the mystical law of human nature that impels exalted feeling to rhythmical expression, for the fervor of the Oriental temperament, the joy of the uplift from Pagan darkness into Christian experience. Remember that the new enthusiasm centered in Christ's person, involving an advance, from the prophetic Messiah of the Psalter to the living Christ of experience, in the song as well as in the heart.

The situation in these primitive little communities doubtless finds an analogy in the actual planting of Christianity in Oriental mission fields of to-day. When the question of restricting sacred song to the Psalms was being fought out in the Assembly of the Free Church of Scotland in the early eighteen seventies, none opposed it more warmly than the missionaries. One of them, Dr. Wilson, illuminated the situation in India:

"Any violence done to the liberty of Christian praise would, if absolute, seriously affect my conscience, having to deal with the incipiency of the Christian Church among the two hundred millions of the inhabitants of India. I could not be a party to offending in this matter the little ones—the converts, who themselves compose and sing their hymns to Christ, both publicly and privately." [8]

Some such native strains may very well have broken out in the free and informal assembly in Gentile churches; just as in the equally free and exalted atmosphere of our own early Western revivals, ejaculations and snatches of song and rhymed refrains were drawn out in the camp-meetings; some of the more effective passing into the revival song books, where they may still be read. In the Gentile churches the emotional and artless songs would be more ephemeral, overshadowed by the glamor of the inspirational songs so soon to flood the assemblies.

2. *The Inspirational Hymn*

We have been reading between the lines. It so happened that the development of psalmody St. Paul pictured first was not along normal channels, but along that of spiritual possession and spiritual gifts, which started at Pentecost. These, as renewed in some Gentile churches, produced the exceptional inspirational singing just referred to.

At the date of his description of the agitated assembly at Corinth (I Cor. xiv) the consciousness of possessing spiritual gifts had spread widely, and the impulse to express them was compelling.

"What happens, brethren? When ye come together every one of you hath a psalm, hath a teaching, hath a revelation, hath a tongue, hath an interpretation. Let all things be done unto edifying."

The Apostle does not deny the reality of the gifts. He does not question the impulse. He is a chairman amid a confusion of voices, calling the meeting to order. How like he is to Jonathan Edwards trying to regulate the outbreaks of the Great Awakening! Finding "something very beautiful" "when many under great religious Affections, are earnestly speaking together in various Parts of a Company," "provided they don't speak so many as to drown each other's Voices, that none can hear what any say." [9]

"Every one of you hath a psalm" (or something other), the Apostle says in his dismay at the superfluity. The Spirit sowed the seed, and, as the poet says,

> "Most can raise the flowers now,
> For all have got the seed."

One can see some rapt figure rising to utter a song that stirs every heart, and then watch the moved hearers hurrying home to try their own hands at writing psalms for the next meeting; until the assemblies come to resemble those eighteenth century hymn-competitions in the Welsh revival.

This charismatic psalmody was sometimes a speaking with tongues and could never have been congregational song. We get an illustration of its performance in the extraordinary movement to revive the "gifts" in Edward Irving's Regent Square congregation in the early eighteen thirties. The gifted were under some strong compulsion and sincerely believed it to be that of God's Spirit. In any case the human reaction would be much the same.

In exercising the gift their voices attained an unnatural intensity and sweetness, their utterance an extreme rapidity in words often unintelligible, and the unmusical developed a gift of melody. The whole personality took on a complete abstraction from time and place. Even an observer might have felt himself (some did) back in the Corinth of St. Paul.[10]

I suppose the inspirational song was called a "psalm" because it suggested an Old Testament Psalm as a model or a source or may be as emphasizing a community of inspiration. But the logic of the situation as well as the context itself requires us to hold that the psalm brought to the Corinthian assembly was not a canonical one, but a fresh composition, the product in each case of the individual gift of the disciple who made it. No inspiration of any sort, not even the fine frenzy of a poet, least of all a miraculous gift, is required to recite a Scripture Psalm at a religious meeting. The contention that the new gift of psalmody to the Gentile churches brought no more than that seems, to me at least, like a failure to interpret a historical occasion.

In the Corinthian assemblies the gift of psalmody was either the best of the charismatic endowments, or else the most conspicuous, for St. Paul names it first.

This precedence among God's gifts in times of spiritual revival it has retained ever since:—in the Lutheran Reformation at Wittenberg and beyond, in the Calvinistic Reformation in Switzerland and France, in the Methodist and Evangelical revival in England and Wales, and in the Great Awakening that swept the American colonies off their feet. At the beginning of the Awakening it was the outbreak of singing, especially of processions of young people singing along roads and streets, that drew out the first reproaches from that eminent moderate, Charles Chauncey.[11] Jonathan Edwards, so proud of the earlier attainments of his Northampton flock in psalmody as to print in a book[12] the fact that the Men carry "regularly and well, *three Parts of Musick*, and the Women a Part by themselves," mentions that at the inception of the revival there in 1735, "Our publick *Praises* were then greatly enliven'd; God was then served in our *Psalmody*, in some measure, in the Beauty of Holiness."

3. *The Enrichment of the Hymnody*

It is questionable if any spiritual revival ever left the songs of a church just where it found them.

The Hussite movement left behind it the vernacular hymn and the people's hymn book; the Lutheran left behind it the German hymnody; the Calvinistic left behind it the metrical Psalm; the Wesleyan left behind it the evangelistic hymn, and shared with the Evangelical side of the revival in creating the hymn of Christian experience; the Great Awakening overcame the prejudice against human composures and changed the churches that it affected from being Psalm singers into hymn-singing churches; the Moody and Sankey campaigns left behind them the "gospel hymn."

What did the early outpouring of heavenly "gifts" leave behind it?

We cannot indicate any actual deposit as we can in the case of later revivals. But it would be hard to believe that it did not leave behind some enrichment of the body of the hymnody itself. The high esteem felt for the gifts make it inconceivable that the favored psalms, those that touched the heart, were allowed to lapse into neglect. They would be treasured in the memory of some, and might pass into the common possession of the Church. I shall deal later with a suggestion that the spiritual odes St. Paul recommended for singing, a few years afterward, may refer to the "Spirit-given" psalms surviving from the revival.

V. St. Paul's Theory of Hymnody

The "gifts" were a passing phenomenon. The excitement passed, as it must if life is to go on. One and another gift failed, until none was exhibited. Even Corinth was in the same position as those other places in which the church gatherings had been maintained steadily but without any consciousness of spiritual endowments.

Psalmody had been a gift. It was now to be established as a permanent ordinance in the assemblies of the brethren.

St. Paul's casual references suggest that the usual assemblies were of two sorts:

(1) His "when ye come together . . . let all things be done unto edifying" (the passage we have been studying) implies an open meeting, free and informal, for the edification of Christians and the instruction of any brought in from outside. Any one is at liberty to offer his contribution: even the uninstructed could respond with his "Amen." (2) His "when ye come together to eat," in I Cor. xi, 33, refers to an assembly for the common meal followed by the Communion, which must have been restricted to the brethren.

St. Paul's dealings with the inspirational song had been specific enough. Did he have views equally definite about the Christian song which is not a day's wonder but our daily food? Did he have a theory of church song?

These questions are answered in two passages in which, say about A. D. 60, he concerns himself with the subject; Ephesians v, 18-20, and Colossians iii, 16, 17. They both deal less by way of description of what was as in anxiety for what might be. And they are thus the Apostolic ideal, and hence our charter, of Christian song.

Take first the passage in Ephesians.

Were it not for the silence of expositors I should have thought it refers obviously to the hymnody of the Love-Feast and Communion:

"*So do not show yourselves senseless* (unsensing

the difference between a pagan and a Christian feast, not discerning the Lord's body), *but understand what is according to Christ's appointment. And do not get drunk with the wine* (as at Corinth). *That is excess. But be filled with the Spirit, speaking responsively in psalms and hymns and spiritual odes, singing vocally with music in your hearts to the Lord: giving thanks throughout in the Name of our Lord Jesus Christ* (as He did at the Supper) *to God the Father.*"

The "submitting yourselves one to another," that follows, is perhaps a rubric in the interests of decency and order at the feast as a symbol of the deeper restraints immediately enjoined.

So much for St. Paul's conception of festal and Communion song,—its source in the Spirit, its enthusiasm also spiritual as against bodily excitement, its note of thanksgiving "always" as its criterion.

This glad note of thanksgiving rings true to Christ's institution of the Supper, from the blessing of the bread and the thanks before the cup to the Great Thanksgiving at the end. It passed into the Communion as observed in *The Teaching of the Apostles* and into the early Greek liturgies, but somehow it dropped out of the Roman Mass. It resounded in Calvin's *The Manner of the Lord's Supper*, which fairly thrills with gratitude. The Communion Office of *The Book of Common Prayer* gives a post-Communion prayer of thanks and shifts the "Gloria in excelsis" from its position in earlier liturgies to form a Great Thanksgiving at the close.

In Knox's Liturgy the intrusion of a long homily and the severe fencing of the Table perhaps quench the spirit of thanksgiving in tender hearts, but the service closes with the 103rd or some other Psalm of thanksgiving. In the Westminster and American Directories for Worship the order for the Communion is too much given up to rigorous self-examination and warning that come too late and mar the occasion. Surely we ought to have examined ourselves before coming there. But at the end the Minister is "to give solemn thanks to God, for His rich mercy and invaluable goodness;" a tardy but a very lovely phrase.

Perhaps, if Presbyterians had adopted the designation of "The Eucharist," favored by the late Dr. Archibald Hodge, the festival character of the sacrament and the eucharistic quality of its hymnody would have been made more prominent. For it is a matter of observation that in Churches long foregoing the observance of the Christian Year, there develops a tendency to make the Communion service a surreptitious observance of Good Friday.

We turn to the passage in Colossians:

"Let the word of Christ dwell in your hearts, enriching you in all wisdom; teaching and admonishing one another with psalms and hymns and spiritual odes, singing with grace in your hearts unto

God. And whatever ye do, in word or deed, do all in the Name of the Lord Jesus, offering thanksgivings to God the Father through Him.

Here again the eucharistic feature of Christian song is carefully conserved not only as its essential but as the actual spiritual atmosphere which envelops it. But the Apostle feels no inconsistency in urging song as a means of mutual edification. He is of course not forecasting a service of praise for the stately basilicas of Constantine's time. He is merely exhorting a little company of people gathered in a humble home for mutual edification. And yet the sort of singing here indicated becomes none the less an authorized form of church song; and every theory of hymnody must wrestle with it or give it lodgment.

Some of us recall an older type of divine in our pulpits who announced each hymn with the formula, "Let us now sing to the praise and glory of Almighty God the —th hymn," and then would perhaps go on to read "Hasten, sinner, to be wise." The Apostle is more candid: "Let us admonish one another with the hymn,

> " 'Waken, thou that sleepest,
> Arouse thee from the dead:' "

that is to say he gives full approval to the Hymn of Edification as a form of Christian song.

Its characteristics are clearly indicated. It is a gospel song. A melody first of all in hearts in which the word of Christ dwells richly, and then a lyrical expression of that inward experience, fitted to be a messenger of grace from heart to heart. Its two special functions singled out, teaching and admonition, are the two happening to be appropriate,—its teaching power in view of the Colossian heresy, its admonitory power in view of the ethical situation.

But the feature of Christian song that stands out most vividly in this passage is its essential individualism. We talk of social singing and community singing in terms of our collective impression. St. Paul seems to see each singer apart, "teaching and admonishing one another." This is because Christian song is to him a purely spiritual function, the natural expression of a heart filled with the Spirit. In his concern that song should flourish among the Colossians he did not exhort them to form music classes but to deepen the spiritual life. And if our Christian song is spiritual, it also must be fundamentally individualistic.

To this conception of it we shall no doubt have to submit our own theories of church song. It is not an ordinance that resides in the sanctuary waiting till a congregation gather to exercise it. It is a spiritual gift which each Christian brings to the sanctuary and contributes to a common song of spiritual fellowship.

VI. The Materials of the Song

1. *The Apostolic Hymn Book*

We have postponed till now any consideration of the poetical materials the Apostle recommended, "Psalms and hymns and spiritual odes": a phrase he liked so well that, having used it in one letter, he repeated it in the other with the precision of a formula.

"We cannot for a moment," Dr. McPherson warns us, "suppose that there is any suggestion of a collection of pieces for use in the public gatherings of Christians." [13]

But what could such a collocation of words mean to humble Christians who were not philologists unless they had at hand something corresponding to it, something by way of a repertory of psalms, hymns and odes? Moreover the Epistle to Colossæ was written to undermine the influence of certain teachers there, once regarded as Gnostics, but whom the latest scholarship supposes to be Judaizers. The Apostle proposes supplementary songs because of their teaching and admonitory power to meet the situation. But what songs? Songs are quite as effective to incite immorality as high living; and good carriers of heresy as well as orthodoxy. Had this urgent protagonist of singing really neglected to provide these ignorant people with hymns of the right sort?

What would a repertory of such contain? A variety, evidently—psalms, hymns and spiritual odes. Psalms from the Septuagint, one would say, although on the only other occasion on which St. Paul mentioned "a psalm," it was one of the new compositions brought into the assembly at Corinth. Some of these must have survived. Then there were Jewish-Christian psalms, if only the three preserved yet by St. Luke. As for hymns,—in so far as St. Paul thought in Greek, he would have in mind songs of direct praise to a God or hero, and would refer here to such "hymns offered to Christ as unto a God" as Pliny's witness heard in Bithynia somewhat later. What the Apostle meant by Spiritual odes we know well enough. And it matters little whether we translate his phrase as Spirit-given songs, or songs composed by Spiritual men, or songs of the Spiritual life, so long as we capitalize the "S."

There was thus a situation that clearly called for a collection of authorized songs, and already a wide range and a considerable variety in the available materials.

It has not been so long since the suggestion of an apostolic hymn book seemed to Dr. McPherson an idle hypothesis, and to others a fabrication to support some theory of liturgical progress in the first century. But we know now that the production and circulation of documents was more facile than we had supposed.

An unforeseen turn to the question was given in 1909 when Dr. Rendel Harris announced the discovery of "An early Christian hymn book." It is a collection of "private psalms," originally Greek, contained in a fifteenth or sixteenth century Syriac MS., bound in with the pre-Christian *Psalms of Solomon* and entitled *The Odes of Solomon*. In this connection our prepossessions count for no more than in the case of the *Didache*, whose discovery proved vexing to many liturgical theorists. And most of us are in the hands of the few specialists accustomed to handle similar documents and who have proved their right to draw conclusions from them.

Mrs. Gibson, who has proved hers so abundantly, ventures a hypothesis that makes the *Odes* earlier than *Ephesians*, and might imply their actual identity with the "odes" of that epistle.[14] Dr. Harris himself had dated them as of the last quarter of the first century; and, after all criticisms are in, maintains that they fall scarcely, if at all, outside the limits of New Testament composition.[15] Harnack dates them at the end of the first century.

That the *Odes* are Christian, originally or as worked over from a Jewish text, seems obvious, with so many allusions to articles of the faith and the clear note of joy in Christ's salvation. But it seems a detached Christianity, proceeding at a high elevation by the mystic way, yet not without some relation to the type of thought St. John made apostolic.

The unfailing "Hallelujah!" in every ode connotes a song book. The whole situation suggests the probability, or, if preferred, the possibility, that we are at last in actual possession of a hymn book of apostolic times. It seems like a materialization in our hands of the stuff that dreams were made on.

As to what phase of Christianity the *Odes* represent, by what party within the Church or at its borders the hymns were used, there is not now and perhaps never will be full agreement. To the mystically inclined they will seem Catholic, and to the sacramentally inclined as sadly lacking in the rudiments. What St. Paul would think of them we can only imagine. We have no warrant certainly to assume that these mystical hymns represent the normal content of an apostolic hymn book, or that they fulfill the type of psalm and ode with whose power to teach the truth and confirm the right St. Paul was so deeply impressed.

2. *The Hymns Quoted in the Epistles*

In that respect we can find firmer ground in his own letters.

Narrowing our survey at first to poetical quotations whose source is unnamed, three especially sound as if they might have come from the apostolic hymn book.

(a) In Ephesians v, 14, there is a quotation whose very *locus* is suggestive, for it immediately precedes the injunction to sing hymns and odes.

"Wherefore one says:

> " 'Thou that sleepest, waken!
> Rouse thee out of death,
> That Christ may be thy Light!' "

The context, the words and the best opinion, at least as far back as Origen, favor regarding this as a quotation of a current hymn; part of a baptismal hymn, it may be.

(b) In I Timothy iii, 16:

> [Who was] "Manifest in flesh,
> Justified in spirit,
> Visible to angels;
> Preached among the nations,
> Believed on in the world,
> Taken up to glory."

A quotation whose context would supply the grammatical subject. Manifestly poetry, with its parallelism of six balanced clauses, of which each triplet forms a climax; and if a quotation of Christian verse, what indeed, if not a hymn?

(c) In II Timothy ii, 11-13: "Faithful is the saying,

> " 'If we have died with Him, we shall also live with Him;
> If we endure with Him, we shall also reign with Him;
> If we deny Him, He too will deny us;
> If we are faithless, He abideth faithful;
> Since He cannot deny Himself.' "

Here we have the same parallelism, an arrangement in couplet and refrain, and an introduction suggesting a familiar quotation.

3. *St. Paul as a Hymn Writer*

But I think we may go further. We have not made enough of St. Paul's declaration, "I will sing praise with the Spirit and with the understanding also" (I Cor. xiv, 15), as expressing what it must mean in its immediate context, his consciousness of possessing a gift for hymn writing and his intention to exercise it.

And I venture to give my personal reaction to the Pauline letters, accompanied by the confession that it is not evidence.

They leave an impression of one whose high-strung temperament and exalted mood dwelt habitually in that atmosphere of light and color with which a spiritual imagination clothes experience. And of one also whose turn for rhetorical expression, half-unconsciously even, transmuted his thoughts and feelings into rhythmical phrases and nicely balanced formularies; staying with him, as such things will, the familiar possession of his mind, pulses of melody in his heart. We see just the same thing in Horatius Bonar, except that Bonar's obsession with the Church as the widowed bride of an absent Christ makes his hymns pathetic while the apostle's joy in the Church as the body of an indwelling Christ makes his eucharistic.

And I think that is why St. Paul's letters break forth so frequently yet so unexpectedly, so liturgically and yet so spontaneously, into rhythmical ascriptions and doxologies. They contain also more extended passages whose exalted rhetoric has a song-like effect that may well be an echo of his own hymns. Who will say that the opening of *Ephesians* itself, "Blessed be God and the Father of our Lord Jesus Christ," with its careful craftmanship and its thrice-sounded refrain, "Unto the praise of His glory," is not an actual transcript of one of his own hymns?

The so-called Hymn of Love that fills I Corinthians xiii is no hymn in the congregational sense. It is the more striking for being inserted in the middle of the discussion of the spiritual gifts. Dean Stanley pictures the amanuensis pausing to look up at the apostle's face for an explanation of his sudden change of style as he begins to dictate his vision of perfection. The lyric personalities with which the passage opens and closes make it quite as easy to picture the Apostle as having risen in some assembly with a seer's vision and utterance to speak the words, here made a part of the record, as an inspirational psalm, in the Spirit and with the understanding also of heavenly love. In any case it is evidence enough of St. Paul's gift of psalmody.

4. *The Odes of the Apocalypse*

The Apocalypse also contains a considerable number of short odes, some of which are plainly a part of the definite prophecies they are connected with.

But there is in the chapters introductory to the vision (iv-x) a group of songs of a more general character of praise to God and the Lamb. Weizsächer was, I believe, the first to suggest that these earlier odes may be no more than transcripts of traditional hymns originally employed in the current worship of the Church on earth, and has shown impressively how the brief songs of chapters iv and v fit into one another like strophes of a complete ode.[16] This view has found so great favor that it has now reached the encylopedic stage,—by which I mean that we may open our cyclopedias at the word "Hymn," expecting to find these odes recorded among the remains of apostolic hymnody.

Weizsächer's suggestion grew out of his conviction that the delineation of divine service in heaven followed the actual proceedings in the Church on earth: by which he means that the actual order of worship in the assemblies was the framework on which the author of the Apocalypse hung the rich tapestries depicting the worship of heaven.

It may be so. But as soon as you attempt to work out the details of the analogy between the heavenly worship and the simple devotions of the assemblies, as Mr. Lowrie has done,[17] you pass with him into an atmosphere more liturgically developed than the one portrayed by the actual records of the first century.

And in the case of the hymns themselves. Our earthly songs do not seem to fit naturally into the pattern of the tapestry. Would it not have been as inept then as now to represent the elders and the cherubim gathered at the throne as singing the strains of our familiar lyrics? It is of course possible that the Church cherished a group of charismatic songs so high and so sacrosanct that they would seem at home in heaven. But to my feeling at least there is some quality or atmosphere about these odes of the Apocalypse that lifts them above the humanities and suggests a birthright in the heavenlies. They do not sound like songs of worship transmitted from an earthly atmosphere so much as like songs of those who look back or down upon the nations and the Church, and are now enclosed within the vision of God.

Some such instinctive feeling as that just suggested may account for the marked hesitancy of the Church through all the centuries to incorporate these odes of the Apocalypse in her liturgies or to include them among her congregational songs. She has probably felt that they are songs of triumph and not visions out of struggle, the triumph of attainment rather than of faith.

And so, for ourselves also, with no other evidence than the contents of the apocalyptic odes themselves, it may be prudent to regard them as idealizations of the Church's praise, or prophetic suggestions of what it shall be, rather than as transcripts from the apostolic hymn book.

LECTURE TWO

THE RELATION OF THE HYMN TO HOLY SCRIPTURE

LECTURE TWO

THE RELATION OF THE HYMN TO HOLY SCRIPTURE

I. A Question: Around Which the Whole History of Hymnody Turns

In the first lecture I tried to show from the evidence that St. Paul authorized a freely composed Christian hymnody and encouraged the churches under his influence to use it as an enlargement of the ordinance of Psalmody.

To suppose that his proposals were welcomed by the Jewish Christian church at Jerusalem; to claim that St. James, in prescribing psalmody for the merry-hearted, included hymns and odes; to deny that St. Paul's views were fought tooth and nail by the Judaizers in provincial churches; to claim that before the end of the apostolic epoch the whole Church was changed from a Psalm-singing to a hymn-singing church: not any one of these assumptions was a part of our case.

On the contrary the present lecture assumes that St. Paul precipitated an issue: Psalms vs. Hymns, and that it divided the opinion and practice of the Church. Has the Church a right to supersede or even enlarge the hymn book that is of canonical authority? Is it not audacious to supplement inspired Psalms with hand-made hymns? And even if it be lawful is it expedient? That is the issue.

To many of us this question of the relation of our Christian song to Scriptural song has not given much concern, and to others it will seem as in no sense a modern question.

The purpose of this lecture is to show that through each succeeding period of the Church's life this question has always remained a modern question, a case of conscience, a center of agitation; that for centuries after the Reformation a difference of opinion regarding the answer kept the Lutheran and Reformed Churches from worshiping together; that in the early days of American Presbyterianism it led to bitterness and division that were heart-breaking; and that it is still enough of a modern question to prevent our divided Presbyterianism not only from corporate union but from joining together in a hymn to Christ.

The scheme of this lecture is to discover the answers to the question the Church has given from time to time, or, in other words, to follow the fortunes of the Christian Hymn; for the two themes are identical.

II. The New Christian Hymns

It is probable that the histories of early Christian worship that are most technical are least true. In attempting to trace the development of public ceremonial one so easily loses sight of the primary fact that the spread of Christianity was the spread of a devotional conception of the private life, which we have allowed to fade away. The essential thing was the spirit and exercises of worship in the individual and family life; and public worship was at heart an extension of these private devotions.

In this devotional life, if anywhere, Christian song, just because of its spiritual character, must find its springs. And evidently it played a large part in the personal and family life of second and third century Christianity.

At Alexandria, where East and West met, Clement, in his second century *Miscellanies*, pictures vividly the true Gnostic as moving in a very atmosphere of hymnody: "We cultivate our fields, praising; we sail the sea, hymning."[1] The Christian's "whole life is a holy festival. His sacrifices are prayers and praises and Scripture readings before meals, psalms and hymns during meals and before bed, and prayers again during night. By these he unites himself to the heavenly choir."[2] As though by way of example, the famous hymn which Dr. Dexter has made familiar as "Shepherd of tender youth" was appended to his *Instructor* by his own or a later hand.

In North Africa Tertullian makes it an objection to the marriage of a Christian with an unbeliever that they could not sing together. Whereas, if both are Christians, "between the two echo psalms and hymns, each challenging the other which shall better chant to the Lord." [3]

Tertullian was not, like Clement, a writer of hymns. "We have a plenty," he told the Christians whom he would entice from the theater. "Plenty of verses, sentences, songs, proverbs." [4] Some he did not approve of: such as "the hymns of Valentine," not to be rated "a respectable author." [5]

We know at least the names of other writers. The martyred Ignatius wrote a hymn to Christ.[6] Another martyr, Athenogenes, left one as "a kind of farewell gift," that was still circulating in the fourth century.[7] Hippolytus, who came also to be accorded a martyr's halo, is said to have composed a whole book of odes.[8] Dionysius of Alexandria speaks affectionately of "the numerous psalms" of Nepos, an Egyptian bishop, "so dear to a vast number of the faithful." [9]

The very casualness of these scattered allusions shows how wide and free was the atmosphere in which the new hymns were composed and received. An impulse, which canonical Psalms did not satisfy, to render homage to Christ was behind most of them,—a motive that kept on renewing itself. So much so that at the end of the second century, an unnamed defender of the faith against the Arians could point out their unbroken continuity: "So great a number of Christian psalms and odes, composed by the faithful from the very beginning, in which they celebrate Christ, the Word of God, proclaiming Him Very God." [10]

The hymns were in Greek, the language of the Christian community, East and West, except in a group of Syriac churches centering at Edessa. Even at Rome till the end of the second century not only the literature but the ritual was in Greek. The "Kyrie eleison" of the Latin liturgy survives as a living witness to the fact.

Some were modeled on the Septuagint Psalter, and gained the quaint title of "private psalms." Some were "odes," like the "Gloria in excelsis," based on the angels' song. Or the lovely hymn for the lamp-lighting hour, which Keble made familiar as "Hail! gladdening Light of His pure glory poured." It was a relic of household worship that Basil called ancient even in his time.[11]

But a preference for Greek classical meters arose very early. Clement's hymn is an example. So is the metrical acrostic now in the Amherst collection.[12] So, very likely, were "the psalms of a new kind" Epiphanius ascribed to the Egyptian ascetic Hierakas.[13]

There is no room to question that the new hymns were used in public worship. Our earliest report happens to be from outside, due to Pliny's anxiety at the spread of the faith in Bithynia. He describes for the emperor a night service very early in the second century. His witnesses affirm "a custom of meeting before dawn on a stated day, and singing by turn a hymn to Christ as a god." [14] The Bithynians are reported as gathering for a common meal, and this Love Feast gave no doubt especial opportunity for Christian song.

In the *Didache*, where feast and sacrament are still connected, no one could draw the line between them or between prayers, thanksgivings and songs.

Tertullian, describing the Love Feast in North Africa, after it had been separated from the Eucharist, tells us that "after hand-washing and bringing in the lights each is asked to stand forth and sing as he can a hymn to God, either one from Holy Scripture or one of his own composing—a proof of the measure of his drinking.[15]

Clement of Alexandria devotes to the music of the Christian feast a whole chapter of his *Instructor*,[16] which is no more than an amplification of St. Paul's warning to the Corinthians, and shows pagan revelry and spiritual emotion, pagan song and Christian hymnody, still contending unseemly at the gate of an observance ideally so beautiful.

In respect of the Communion itself, Justin Martyr's account of it (in Antioch perhaps at the middle of the second century) says nothing of psalm or hymn, unless such were included in the prayers and thanksgivings offered by the President and responded to by the people. But he had just mentioned the custom in their worship of offering thanks in hymns.[17] Probably the Communion was preceded by a course of psalmody as in the fourth century liturgies. To what extent private psalms entered in we cannot tell.

In Greek, as in Jewish and apostolic worship, there was no clear discrimination of praise and prayer or even singing and reading. Very likely what we call the prayers of fourth century liturgies are transcripts or compilations of earlier Christian psalms. In the *Testament of our Lord* the prayers which offer praise are throughout designated as "Hymns."

III. The Greek Settlement of the Question

Private psalms and Christian odes never won a parity with canonical Psalms, the Church's cherished inheritance of praise. This difference of level was used subtly in proceedings to depose Paul of Samosata, an adventurer who became Bishop of Antioch for a decade from 260. The charge was that he suppressed "the Psalms chanted there in honor of our Lord." His plea was one of confession and avoidance. The psalms he had suppressed "were not the ancient Psalms of David: they were new and the work of new men." [18]

There was indeed growing up in "Catholic" circles a suspicion of the hymn of human composure. It was due in part to jealousy for the supremacy of

Scripture, but yet more to the activity of heretical parties, Gnostics especially, in using hymns as propaganda.

In Edessa, as early as 200, the accomplished Bardesanes had actually composed a rival psalter of 150 psalms; "deserting David's truth and preserving David's numbers," as Ephraim put it.[19] It seems to have been sung in Syriac churches for more than a century. And in that trial of Paul of Samosata it came out that in setting aside the psalms sung in Christ's honor he had not hesitated to substitute a new series sung by female choirs, "composed in his own honor"; whatever that evil-sounding phrase may mean.

Of the hymns of Valentine, a Gnostic who came to Rome in the middle second century, we have already heard Tertullian's opinion. Marcion also came to Rome about the same time to foster his special type of Gnosticism, and it is likely that his "new book of psalms" swelled the number of his followers.[20]

By the fourth century the hymn had become the favorite common carrier of Arian heresy; not only among congregations, but by special "songs for sailors" and "songs for travelers," which "insinuated their pernicious teachings into simple hearts through the charm of their music." [21]

The Church was witnessing an effective demonstration of the teaching power of hymns. It could hardly fail to arouse in the "Catholic" type of mind a conviction that the freely-composed hymn had become a menace.

That conviction throws some light upon the action of the Synod that met at Laodicæa about 363. Its 59th canon, or the undisputed section of it, reads:

"Psalms composed by private men must not be read in the church nor uncanonical books, but only the canonical of the New and Old Testament."

"Read" covers the psalmody as well as the lectionary, since the contemporaneous usage was to recite the psalm by a Reader in sing-song. The congregational participation consisted of responses or a chant-wise recitation of verses somewhat in the manner of the antiphons of the Roman Office.

It was these responses apparently, and anything else in the way of hymns the people were accustomed to sing, that were dealt with in another canon, the 15th, providing that "beside the psalm singers appointed thereto, who mount the ambo and sing out of the book, no others shall sing in church."

Neander[22] and those who follow his lead make this to mean no more than that a member of the congregation is no longer free to start the hymn, as we would say of a prayer-meeting. But there was undoubtedly a movement to get every part of the worship out of the people's hands into those of officiants. The day of church-building had come and the call for a form of service corresponding to the architecture. With trained choristers in the lead the ruder outpourings of an illiterate people would become indecorous. This canon looks like an official approval of the movement to silence the people. And in view of the fact that their part in church song was taken away from them and was put into the hands of the choir, in whose exclusive possession it remains until the present day in the Greek church, it does not seem unreasonable to interpret the canon as meaning just what it says.

And so we get the FIRST, A GREEK CHURCH SETTLEMENT of the question that had been vexing it, the relation of its church song to Scripture; deciding the same by exalting the canonical Psalms to an exclusive place in honor and in use, and explicitly forbidding the introduction of psalms of human composition into church worship; and prohibiting the people from taking any part in the church song except as listeners to those appointed to render it.

Both the scope and the effectiveness of this ban put upon "private psalms" are debatable. Certainly it did not hinder the development of an extensive Greek hymnody. And it is hard to see how a small local synod could have done more than establish a precedent. Dr. Batiffol, the accomplished historian of the *Roman Breviary*, regards its action as final: "private psalms were banished from Catholic liturgical use." [23] He is perhaps thinking only of such as had wormed their way into the prescribed course of Psalmody proper that paralleled the Lectionary. At most the canon appears to deal only with the sanctities of worship within church walls, and not with popular song or the singing of hymns in gatherings and festivals not covered by the liturgy.

Chrysostom must have thought so. When he came to Constantinople in 398 he did not hesitate to meet the Arians with their own weapons and to imitate their processions of singers by organizing rival processions trained to sing orthodox hymns specially composed for them. He must have felt that the springs of sacred song were not choked, and that there were channels through which it might still flow.[24]

IV. The Latin Settlement

The Greek hymn passes out of the hands of the people, and so beyond the scope of these lectures. We turn now to the Latin hymn.

Dr. Warfield used to say that there is a real sense in which North Africa is the mother of us all.[25] She was certainly the mother of the Western Church. And the Romanizing process that changed her language from Greek to Latin made Latin the mother tongue of that Church.[26] It was at Carthage, not Rome, that the Psalms were first chanted in Latin, as they are still throughout the Roman communion. The Septuagint had been roughly translated, and the roll containing the Psalter furnished the text.

The great Tertullian had ceased to write in Greek by 213.[27] That passionate heart did not turn to hymn writing, which was as well, in view of the virtuosity of his style. There is no tradition of Latin hymns as yet at Carthage.

Their *writing* began in the fourth century with Hilary in his remote Gallic diocese. He made a book of them for his people. Jerome tells us how he complained of finding the Gauls unteachable in sacred song.[28] He was a theologian, and it may be overstrained its teaching office.

Their *singing* waited upon Ambrose of Milan, whose effective hymns were practically a new creation. They make him the father of Latin hymnody and the real inaugurator of modern hymnody in every tongue.

St. Augustine's *Confessions* have made familiar to us all the first hearing of Ambrose's hymns, in defending the faith against an Arian court. In 385 he had refused to yield the new basilica at Milan to the dowager empress Justina. She renewed her demand a year later, when the alarm spread that not only the church but Ambrose's person were to be seized. Taking refuge in the basilica, he was surrounded by a concourse of the faithful, who for some days and nights guarded both church and bishop against the imperial troops. Ambrose organized his affectionate flock into a band of constant worshipers, preaching and arranging a course of devotions, and training them to sing his hymns, "lest the people wax faint through the tediousness of sorrow."

What an opportunity to try out his ideals of Christian song! He so used it as to make Milan a focal point in the history of the hymn. It gathers up the lines of development we have been studying, on the one side, and on the other the lines on which modern hymnody still proceeds.

What was new at Milan, apart from the antiphonal singing Ambrose brought over from the East, was the hymns themselves. The assembly, the fervor, the hymnody of edification, were apostolic,—the hymns were Ambrosian.

Their characteristic was in being composed in Latin meter, but so were Hilary's. Their distinction was in using the metrical form so successfully as to make it inevitable. Even to-day in our remote American Protestantism, when we use the word "hymn" in common speech we are thinking of the Ambrosian hymn.

Ambrose's difficulty lay in the artificiality of classical meters as a mold in which to pour Christian emotion. He chose the simplest of lyric meters, a strophe of four iambic dimeters,—a stanza of four eight-syllabled lines. So wisely that allowing for the gradual change from metrical to word accent, his chosen meter was almost invariably used in Latin hymns till the eleventh century, and is the familiar Long Meter of our present-day books.

St. Augustine's references to Ambrose's hymns show how they struck a contemporary. They won also the sincerest flattery of imitation, becoming the nucleus of a body of "Ambrosiani," which still keeps its place in the *Roman Breviary*.

The popular hymn singing itself Ambrose set up at Milan spread rather quickly through Italy and even Gaul, and gave some promise of establishing itself as a permanent ordinance. Unfortunately it was fated to contract from the volume of congregational song to the narrowness of monastic devotion and of priestly soliloquy.

This is what happened.

The special chance to introduce popular hymn singing came when the morning and evening "hours of prayer" were turning into a church service. Two such "hours" had been observed privately by Christians from the first,—at the breaking of dawn and at lighting the household lamps. These are the primitive "Canonical Hours," matins and vespers. In addition Daniel's "three times a day" influenced the devout, and the three hours as indicated in *Acts*, happening to coincide with the divisions of the civil day, were also consecrated by prayer.[29] This was still in private. But by the middle of the fourth century the churches were being opened for saying these daily offices under direction of the clergy. Why should the new basilicas stand empty while prayers and Psalms were recited outside? And then there was the urge of the devotional intensity marking the groups of ascetics formed in the congregations. They were not yet set apart from common life, but already their specialty lay in emphasizing the "hours" set apart from common day.

These had become so many, it seemed expedient to assign to each one its special Psalms, to avoid repetition and monotony. An *Ordo Psallendi* thus developed. But the multiplication of services that made the *Ordo* necessary also made it impossible for most people to attend them. They were left to ascetics and the clergy.

When somewhat later the ascetics deserted the congregations for a life of prayer in the wilderness, they took with them the *Ordo Psallendi* and such Ambrosian hymnody as was included, and left behind nothing more than the obligation of the clergy to read the Daily Office which still edifies, or it may be burdens, the Roman Catholic priesthood.[30]

And so it happened that the Ambrosian hymns themselves, and the singing of hymns Ambrose had set up at Milan, passed out of the people's lives, and became the exclusive possession of the clergy. They were sung only by the monks in their communities or the choirs of monastic churches: outside they were read in private by secular priests.

In both community and church the staple of the monastic Office was the orderly cantillation of the canonical Psalms. Whether they might be supplemented by metrical hymns, more suggestive of the hour or day or season being observed, was a question that would not be stilled, a case of conscience,—the old question of the supremacy of Scripture in praise: and behind it the ascetic spirit that glories in the clean hearth and the rigor of the game.

The decision lay with the monks as most concerned. It was practically settled when early in the sixth century Benedict of Nursia issued his famous "Rule," reducing a monk's life to clocklike regularity. He made hymn singing a part of it, adopted the *Ambrosiani* and distributed them among the various Hours.[31] His example was followed by Aurelian, Bishop of Arles. And in 567 a Council at Tours went further, saying, "There are writers beside St. Ambrose whose hymns are beautiful enough to deserve singing, and should be received"; provided the author's name is set forth in each case.

But there was strong opposition. The Ambrosian hymns were not received at Rome, and her influence was against them for centuries. In Spain a small council at Braga in 563 had forbidden the singing in church of anything "poetical" except Scripture songs. This hostility must have lingered long in Spain, for in 633 the Council of Toledo found it necessary to show cause why hymns should be allowed.

It is impossible to read its findings without a smile at the circles in which progress moves; for a thousand and more years afterward in far-off England young Isaac Watts was to confront just the same situation, to meet it with the same impatience with the Psalm singers and just the same arguments for human hymns as were exhibited at Toledo.

"We possess," it was there declared, "some hymns composed to the praise of God, the Apostles and the martyrs, such as those of the Blessed Doctors Hilary and Ambrose. And these are rejected by certain people on the pretext that nothing should be received into the liturgy except the text of Holy Scripture only. What do these people say of 'Gloria Patri'? And what of 'Gloria in excelsis'? And what of the lessons read in the Office? And of the prayers? There is then no more ground for condemning the hymns than the prayers, and in this matter Gaul and Spain ought to observe the same custom."

And so, by the seventh century, in Spain as well as in Gaul the Ambrosian hymn had won its way into the Daily Office; and in Ireland also, as a surviving copy of the *Bangor Antiphonary* (now appropriately kept at Milan) testifies. To us, who associate them especially with the *Roman Breviary*, it is hard to realize the five centuries that elapsed during which Rome stood firm for the exclusive use of "the Bible only" as church song. It thus anticipated the position which some of us may have imagined was first taken by John Calvin. Not until the end of the twelfth century were hymns of human composure admitted into the Office as sung at Rome,[32] and only then was their victory complete.

But what a victory! The introduction of hymns at Rome probably involved little more than their singing by the monks attached to the basilicas. How far a remove from Ambrose's project of an evening and morning prayer at which the plain people could do their own singing!

Thus we have the SECOND, the LATIN CHURCH SETTLEMENT of the vexed question of the relation of hymns to Holy Scripture.

The canonical Psalms are the source of the subject-matter of praise both in the Daily Office and the Mass. Scriptural canticles and a few ancient prose hymns from the Greek are also used in the liturgy. But the Rule of Benedict, providing for the chanting of the entire Psalter from beginning to end within each week of the year, makes the Psalms supreme if only for the overshadowing of their preponderating bulk, to say nothing of the loyalty to Scripture which such a Rule attests. In this daily diet of psalmody a limited number of approved metrical hymns of human composure are inserted at fixed points of the Office; serving to connect the Psalms with the hour, the day, or the season of the Christian Year.[33] After the ninth century the provision was somewhat enlarged by admitting some hymns of freer meter, called Sequences,[34] into the

Mass, which had become the principal service of parish churches.

The actual singing in churches, whether monastic or parochial, was to be done by officiants in the choir. For participation by the congregation in the nave there was no provision whatever and no opportunity.

V. The Lutheran Settlement

Such was substantially the situation as the Reformation dawned in Germany.

No one was more familiar with it than Martin Luther, an Augustinian monk. No one was better equipped to sponsor a Protestant movement to restore the hymn to the people: to restore it to its right place in worship by first making it a messenger of the gospel to men's hearts. And he had the precedent and encouragement of the successful rise of a popular hymnody in the Hussite revival.

Luther brought away from the convent a real love for the hymns and plain song of the Daily Office. So real that he lacked heart to "banish the Latin language from divine service" altogether, for the sake of "so much fine music and hymnody the Latin has." [35] Nevertheless his great work lay in freeing the hymn from its shackling Latinity, and developing a vernacular hymnody more on the lines of German folk song.

He had first to find the hymns or make them.

"We lack poets, or else they are not known, who can write for us godly spiritual songs, as Paul calls them. Should there be any German poets, I say this to stimulate them." [36] Luther thus made himself responsible for the copious production of German hymns. Perhaps his choice of "spiritual songs" from St. Paul's trio helped to fix upon them their characteristic concern with inward experience.

The best he could do at the moment was to point out two or three of the rather rude and not always decorous current songs as "grave enough." [37] His little booklet of 1524 had only eight hymns: his last hymn book of 1545 had 101, 35 by himself.

Luther's hymns, so long disregarded in Reformed Churches, are nevertheless the foundation of Protestant song. They are as plain as Ambrose's, with more metrical variety but hardly poetic. With him the hymn becomes evangelical, and it is cheerful by intention. "When we sing," he said with customary good sense, "both heart and mind should be cheerful and merry." [38] His hymns belong mostly to St. Paul's hymnody of edification.[39]

From the hymn book prefaces and the discursive but very edifying liturgical writings, we can shape without difficulty the THIRD, the LUTHERAN SETTLEMENT of the relation of hymns to Scripture.

It retained canonical Psalmody as a distinctive ordinance, as in the Latin Church. "Let the entire Psalter, distributed into parts, remain in use at the morning and evening service."[40] He of course relieved the congregation of the obligation to go through the Psalter in a week in the immensely protracted lengths of the "parts" of the Daily Office; which had rested on the Roman clergy. This obligation, in his plain way, Luther called "a donkey's burden." He expected the Psalms to be *sung* where practicable, and was quite willing they be sung in the customary Latin. In the schools the boys are "to sing some Psalms in Latin every morning."[41]

The Lutheran settlement appropriated the metrical hymn side by side with the Psalm, as found in the Latin Office. The inventor of our metrical hymn was Ambrose, not Luther. But he took it away from the closed hands of clergy and choristers and put it into the hands of the people. He translated it into their tongue and freed it from all the rubrical restrictions of office books. Not by comparing Roman and Lutheran liturgies do we come upon Luther's dealings with the hymn. He took it out of liturgies and put it into people's hearts and homes, that when they had learned it and loved it they might bring it to the church and sing it together. He revived, that is to say, St. Paul's conception of hymnody as a spiritual function.

It is important to understand how these dealings with the hymn, so directly opposite to those of later reformers, were nevertheless made to accord in Luther's own thinking with his governing liturgical canon,—the supremacy of the Scriptures in church worship.

(a) He found his authority for composing and using spiritual songs in St. Paul's coupling them with Psalms and in the practice of the Apostolic Church:[42] the stand-point incidentally of our first lecture.

(b) He acknowledged that such authority and precedent may be rightly claimed "in an especial manner in respect of Psalms," and therefore (note the logic) he favored "the attempt to transform a Psalm into a hymn," retaining its sense but passing by "certain forms of expression and employing other suitable ones."[43] Thus he anticipated Dr. Watts' *The Psalms of David imitated*.

(c) The thought that had troubled the early Church and was to divide the Protestant, that the provision of an inspired book of song precluded the intrusion of human composures, found no lodgment in Luther's mind. To prevent its lodging in any other's he calls "the songs of holy writ to witness that patriarchs and prophets composed original hymns," and therefore a modern reformer and his friends who do likewise should "not be looked upon as innovators" but as following in the train of these ancient worthies.

(d) But the vital connection of the Lutheran hymn with the Bible is through its theme and subject-matter. The evangelical content of the hymn meant everything to Luther. "What I wish," he wrote his friend Spalatin, "is to make German hymns for the people, that the Word of God may dwell in their hearts by means of song also." Upon that ideal the whole edifice of the new hymnody rested. Like everything in Lutheran worship it illustrated the conviction of its great founder that the supremacy of Scripture in Christian worship means that the worship must be a setting forth of Christ's gospel.

From this we are now to turn to the fathers of the Reformed Churches, whose reverence for the same Bible led them not only to reject the Lutheran hymnody but to banish the hymn of human composure from the whole breadth of the Reformed world.

VI. The Calvinistic Settlement

We think of Zwingli and Calvin as taking Luther's place in the Churches we have agreed to call "Reformed." The name is unhappy. It was Luther, with his love of the Latin Church, who contemplated reforming it. Whereas Zwingli and Calvin had the vision of a primitive Church restored rather than an existing Church reformed.

But in discussing Calvin's settlement of church praise we must remember that his work at Geneva belongs to the second period of the Swiss Reformation, and was constructive, not iconoclastic.

When he comes on the scene a model of worship

had been set up by Zwingli for the German-speaking cantons. In his church at Zurich, stripped and whitewashed, the worshipers were auditors, except for a few responses, the Creed, Gloria, and a recited Psalm. These "ceremonies" were his concession to human weakness, but singing was not among them. Did Zwingli contemplate the anomaly of a religion without music? His most competent biographer thinks not.[44] The facts are against him. There was no music at Zurich for seventy years. And it is the facts that are Calvin's background.

At Geneva before Calvin came in July, 1536, they were using an order of worship made by Farel, an evangelist from German-speaking Berne to French-speaking cantons. Here, too, there was no singing, probably out of deference to Berne. But there was indeed nothing in French to sing.

After a survey of the situation Calvin drew up his "Essentials of a well-ordered Church," giving prominence to the Psalms "we desire to be sung in church," for these three reasons:

1. The example of the ancient Church and St. Paul's testimony.

2. The warmth and uplift they would bring to our prayers, now so cold.

3. The discovery of what benefit and consolation the pope and his partisans have deprived the Church, by appropriating the Psalms to be mumbled between them without understanding.[45]

Calvin's thought was to begin by training the children to sing prose Psalms to some sober ecclesiastical chant; the people listening till they could grow accustomed to use their own voices in church. The scheme was rather in the air; Calvin's influence was waning and political considerations induced the Council to adhere to the church usages Berne was pressing upon Geneva. This to Calvin meant the supremacy of State over Church. Rather than yield he suffered banishment.

It is well to note that in his humiliation and his appreciation of the need of complaisance, Calvin none the less made it the *sine qua non* of his return to Geneva that the singing of Psalms be made a part of public worship.[46] This purpose, indomitable and perhaps not without a touch of the heroic, is the historical basis on which the whole structure of Metrical Psalmody rests.

Calvin's banishment brought him at Strasburg the opportunity of hearing the Germans sing Luther's hymns; and convinced him that French Psalms could just as well be turned into modern meters and set to congregational tunes. He soon had his little flock of French refugees there singing after some fashion and in 1539 printed a little psalm book for them. In direct contrast with Luther's first booklet, its contents, excepting the Creed, were entirely Biblical: 17 Psalms in meter and one in prose, "Nunc dimittis" and the Commandments versified.

Calvin was back in Geneva by 1541, and could

have anything he wanted, even Psalm singing. He proceeded to enlarge and improve his little Strasburg book. But his standard was so high that twenty-one years passed before he fulfilled his purpose to provide his people with a complete metrical version of the Scripture Psalms.[47]

We have then the FOURTH, the CALVINISTIC SETTLEMENT of the relation of the hymn to Scripture: as conservative as the Judaizers in the Apostolic Church could have wished for, or as was laid down by the Council of Braga in the sixth century.

The hymn of human composure that had been sung so freely in the early Church, that had won so hardly a restricted place in the liturgy of the Latin Church, that had developed so phenomenally in the German Reformation, is now excluded from Reformed worship. The inspired songs of Scripture, substantially the Old Testament Psalter, furnish the exclusive subject-matter of praise. Translated into the vernacular, versified in modern meters, set to congregational tunes, they become the hymns of the Church.

The first question to emerge is whether Calvin aimed to lay down a hard and fast rule binding the Reformed Church for all time?

Undoubtedly all his arrangements at Geneva were by way of exemplifying "a well-ordered Church," and among its essentials, he said, was "the singing of the Psalms" in worship. Just as he insisted on singing against Zwingli's silence, so he emphasized psalmody against Luther's hymnody.

Calvin of course was dealing with a situation rather than the future. Like Luther before him, and practically all the Psalm versifiers after him who disclosed their motives in prefaces, he was nauseated by the unseemly and amorous songs that were corrupting the youth of his country. He was offended just as much by the Latin hymns of the Church, because by his time they had become vehicles of Mariolatry, saint worship and other things he abominated. Obviously then songs of human composure, to say the best of them, were subject to the contagion of levity and heresy.

"What is to be done?" Calvin asks in his preface of 1543.[48] It is, he says:

First: To find songs not only pure but holy.

Second: But none can write them save he who has received the power from God Himself.

Third: "When we have searched all around, here and there, we shall find no songs better or more suitable than the Psalms of David which the Holy Spirit dictated and gave to him."

Fourth: "And therefore, when we sing *them*, we are as sure that God hath put words into our mouths as if He Himself sang with us to exalt His glory."

Expressions so cautious and considerate make us wonder if there were advocates of Lutheran hymnody at Geneva, whom it was prudent to placate.

In any event if Calvin felt more than he expressed, he kept it to himself. No one has produced any assertion that the canonical Psalter was the divinely prescribed hymn book for all time. On the contrary his *Commentary on Colossians* admits that St. Paul's "Psalms and hymns and spiritual odes" covers "all kinds of song," except that "spiritual" excludes "frivolities and trifles." Calvin rested his cause (and won it) not on any divine prescription of the Psalter but on its inspiration. There is no evidence that he had scruples of conscience against the use of human songs. If he had he preferred to propose a counsel of prudence and not a case of conscience.

Most of us are likely to feel now that Calvin's settlement of the matter lacks the finality that comes through comprehensiveness. But now is not then. As a handling of the situation it was masterly. In an emergency it is often the single-track mind that discerns the path ahead and commands the following. Calvin must have read deeply into the French character, and with some foresight of what French Protestants were to go through. If not, he was the unconscious instrument of a clear Providence.

In the Metrical Psalms he gave the people an appealing part of the Bible in their own tongue; which accounts for the thrill of Huguenot psalmody. In the little psalm books he gave it into their own personal possession. The humblest of them might have a copy of his very own: the symbol and vehicle of his personal communion with God.

Some sixty-four editions within four years, supplying Switzerland and peddled through France, show how wide that sense of ownership became, and explain how psalmody became a part of personal life. The metrical Psalter made the Huguenot character. No doubt a character nourished on Old Testament ideals will lack the full symmetry of the gospel. But the Huguenot was a warrior first, called to fight and suffer for his faith. And in singing Psalms he found his confidence and strength. Now that we have seen an idealized pugnacity and a stolid endurance combined in the French soldiery in their war against Germany, we can understand how the Huguenot found no Psalm too militant, no imprecation too severe, against his Lord's enemies.

In the wars of religion the Psalms in meter were the songs of camp and march, the war-cry on the field, the swan song at the martyr's stake.[49]

There was naturally no question of the proper subject-matter of praise when "the Reformed Churches of France" met in Synod in 1559. The Calvinistic settlement was read into the constitution. The bringing of his own psalm book to church by every worshiper was made a part of the discipline.[50] It was a token of the believer's personal share in church song. The injunction to uncover his head while he sang was a token of the dignity of God's Word in song.

VII. Doctor Watts' Settlement

Calvin's standard, "the Bible only" in praise, became a precedent for the Reformed Churches on the continent and in Scotland. Even the Church of England had to give the people a metrical Psalter to bind up with the Prayer Book. Naturally, as is the way of religious precedents, it hardened into a church principle. I have suggested that to us it may not seem a final settlement of the matter. But it was final to those who carried on the Calvinistic Reformation and to generations succeeding them through two centuries.

It was still regarded as final by the immigrants from various shores (except Germany) who laid the foundations of American Protestantism, and until the gospel fervor of the Great Awakening put the matter to question once more. In the Presbyterian Church, most conscious of its Calvinistic inheritance, the issue thus raised passed from the debate on an academic question into a living flame of controversy that scorched kind hearts, broke up parishes, and convulsed the Church. It was only after years of bitterness and disruption that Calvin's settlement of praise was overthrown, and the right to sing hymns of human composure was vindicated.

It ought to enhance our sense of privilege in singing them to remember how hardly that privilege was won. It ought to make us more tolerant toward others to realize that we can only exercise that privilege by turning our own backs on the most distinctive tradition of Reformed worship.

There is no reason for assuming that the body of Reformed Churches actually framed a theory that the inspired Book of Psalms was the divinely prescribed hymn book, or that they ever banned New Testament canticles. But, as things worked out, their practice did confine them to an Old Testament psalmody as rigidly as though prescribed.

And this was to prove the weakness of Psalm singing, the little rift within the lute. For it shut out the church's song from the light of the gospel the pulpit was preaching. It barred even its mention of that Name in which the congregation was praying.

However long delayed, the break with the old Psalmody was bound to come in the interests of spiritual reality. A New Testament Church was bound to resume the new song.

Our immediate concern is with English-speaking Churches.[51] The low estate into which their psalmody had fallen by the end of the seventeenth century, its spiritual indifference, the shocking dilapidation of its music, fairly cried out for a change. What was waited for was a leader willing to incur the reproach of change and capable of furnishing the materials for an evangelical hymnody.

He appeared in the person of Isaac Watts, a minister among the Independents, of marked gifts, who wore the self-confidence of youth like a panoply, and advanced into what he knew would be a fray with full intent of being the aggressor.

And now as to his tactics. He first (1707) showed the feasibility of the new song in a volume of original hymns adapted to the Psalm meters. As an appendix he printed an *Essay towards the Improvement of Christian Psalmody*, proposing a new "System of Praise" that included Psalms, hymns and spiritual songs.

This, in view of the novelty of its terms and of the general adoption of its proposals, must be reckoned the FIFTH, an EVANGELICAL SETTLEMENT of the relation of our hymns to the Bible.

In all fairness it should bear the name of Watts. In the light of its immediate surroundings it was so glaringly original. But, as we discuss it, I think we shall come to feel more and more that to a larger view, it was hardly more than a dislodgment of the Calvinistic settlement in favor of a reaffirmation of Luther's, which was the original evangelical settlement of hymnody.

(a) Watts denied in general that we are under the call, either of God or of Christian prudence, to sing the Bible. Quite the contrary. The Bible is

God's word to us. It is to be received as such and personally appropriated. That being done, our hymns represent, not our repetition of God's word, but our response to it, our word to God. And our word to God can be expressed in the letter of the Bible only in so far as its language can properly be made our own. And thus he laid the ground for the free hymn of human composure, especially evangelical hymns responding to the fullness of God's revelation of Himself in Christ.

(b) In particular Watts denied that the Book of Psalms was either a canonical hymn book for the Christian Church or adapted to its use. It was a Jewish not a Christian book. In a Christian praise book the supremacy must be given to the gospel, not to the Psalms. "Some of 'em are almost opposite to the Spirit of the Gospel; many of them foreign to the State of the New Testament, and widely different to the present Circumstances of Christians." This thought he proceeded to elucidate by exegesis and illustration with a frankness no doubt trying to the lovers of the Psalms. All this was leading up to his conclusion that if we are to make Christian hymns of the Psalms we must first translate them anew; that is to say, rewrite them in the way David would have written them if he had been a Christian and not a Jew, and were a loyal citizen of eighteenth century England.

This he proceeded to do, on his own account, furnishing the churches with his famous *The Psalms of*

David imitated in 1719. I am looking while I write at a presentation copy of that book to his "Hon^d. Uncle," and wondering if any other has been so momentous in the later history of Reformed Churches. It was the bridge across which many of them, including our own, forced their way, half unconsciously, from the restrictions of an imposed Psalmody to the more open country of which Christ is the Light and the Song.

(c) Further, Watts denied the claim of the Metrical Psalm to be the pure word of God. If it be our duty to sing only in the words of Scripture, metrical versions do not fulfill the requirement. The exigencies of rhythm and rhyme make a really faithful rendering of the Hebrew into English verse an impossible thing. Those who wish nothing but the pure word must resort to prose, and must learn the Hebrew music or at least employ the method of chanting practiced in Church of England cathedrals.

The point was a neat one from the contemporaneous point of view. Watts' criticism of the Metrical Psalm is equally valid from the standpoint of modern culture. The English ballad meter, which was the favorite of the old psalm books, was an inadequate medium for transmitting either the form or spirit of Hebrew poetry. If the Psalms are to be read in English, prose couplets are best, and if they are to be sung the method of chanting "practiced in English cathedrals" is the most available.

It was no part of Watts' proposal to give up either

the form or substance of metrical psalmody. He would carry it on not as inspired Scripture but as a department of Christian song whose "sense and materials" were taken from the Bible. And when to this evangelized and modernized Psalter was added a body of hymns of purely human composure, representing our appropriation of the gospel through Christian experience, we get the full terms of Watts' settlement of the relation of Christian song to the Bible.

It worked. Among the humblest Independents first of all; more gradually throughout the Churches that had hitherto stood for "the Bible only." The accommodated Psalms became the recognized standard of Calvinistic orthodoxy. The hymn of human composure won the place alongside from which it has never been dislodged. The twin volumes of "Watts' Psalms and Hymns" made themselves at home in the pews, and represented respectively the Old and New Testaments in praise.

VIII. The Modern Disposition of the Question

The present-day attitude of the Church has not come about in the terms of another formal settlement of the matter but as a natural result of its own experimenting with the double standard of "Psalms and Hymns" set up by Dr. Watts.

When once the divide had been reached, those on whom the obligation or the custom of singing canonical Psalms still pressed were neither fooled nor conciliated by his *Psalms of David imitated.* They stayed, as considerable numbers of them stay apart yet, to praise God according to their conscience. It has been claimed recently that not less than thirteen Reformed communions adhere to the principle of an inspired psalmody. Presumably the Synodical action of 1925 by the United Presbyterians must be regarded as a defection.

But the congregations and communions that admitted human hymns to a parity with divine Psalms did so because the impulse to sing the gospel was more pressing than any duty they felt of singing Psalms. And in practice the evangelical hymns turned out to be more appealing than evangelized Psalms. The new psalmody was a little heavy with its adjustments of prophecy and gospel, its replacements of Israel by Great Britain or "the States." And then it was static, while the hymnody was constantly being freshened with new composures and adjusted to changes in Christian feeling. And so the use of Psalms tended to diminish.

The era of "Psalms and Hymns" gradually merged into an era of "Hymns." As the books labeled on their backs, "Psalms and Hymns" had replaced the *Psalms in meter*, so the "Hymnal" came to replace the "Psalms and Hymns." Some still surviving can remember when the Old School

Presbyterian *Psalms and Hymns* was replaced by the *Hymnal* of 1866; a book futile enough, but a landmark still as the first to ignore the old division into Psalms and hymns.

In modern hymnals such Psalm versions as are retained are kept there generally for their intrinsic worth as hymns, or possibly for some association's sake; but in either case without regard to their fidelity as translations. The fetters, whether of obligation, or of prudence, or of use and wont, that held the Church's songs so close to the letter of Scripture, were in the minds and habits of English-speaking Christians finally severed by Dr. Watts.

Some of the eighteenth century writers seem to have had a feeling that it was proper to relate their hymns to particular passages of Scripture, either as a Psalm-version relates itself to a canonical Psalm, or at least as a sermon relates itself to a text. Of the three "books" of Watts' *Hymns* the first bears the title, "Collected from the Scriptures." The first book of Newton and Cowper's *Olney Hymns* is "On select Texts of Scripture." Even Charles Wesley printed two volumes of *Short Hymns on select passages of Scripture*. But probably this practice was largely occasioned by the general desire of evangelical preachers to find hymns on the text or passage from which they preached, to use as illustrations or enforcements of their sermon.

The Church of Scotland, where the tradition of a Scriptural psalmody was especially tenacious, did endeavor, between the years 1743 and 1781, to cover the new hymnody with the old sanction by applying to it the method of Scripture paraphrasing. After much travail the General Assembly set forth in the latter year its *Translations and Paraphrases, in verse, of several passages of Sacred Scripture*. The hope was of finding common ground where the upholder of Scripture song and the clamorous advocate of the new hymns might dwell together in peace and sing in harmony. It was a vain hope and a poor expedient—largely camouflage. A few of the Paraphrases are still familiar, notably "O God of Bethel, by whose hand" and "Come, let us to the Lord our God." But they abide because good hymns, and few of those who sing them think of relating them to the Scripture they paraphrase.

The modern feeling in these matters involves no special distaste for the practice of paraphrasing a Scripture passage in order to make a hymn, provided the paraphraser can make something that approaches poetry and stimulates devotion. Most congregations enjoy the simplicity of the Tate and Brady "While shepherds watched their flocks by night"; but I dare say they prefer Phillips Brooks' contemplation of the "little town of Bethlehem" from a human point of view. The Communion paraphrase, " 'Twas on that night when doomed to know" is still dear to many Scottish hearts. But a wider public prefers Montgomery's "According to Thy gracious word," in which the singer does not recite but does appropriate the Words of Institution.

The fact is simply that, as this whole matter of the relation of our praise to Scripture stands to-day in the minds and hearts of most of us, the conviction abides that the Christian hymn has by a process of development disassociated itself from that inevitably close connection with the letter of Scripture which it took on at the Calvinistic Reformation. There has been indeed not so much a process of development as a reversion. To most of us the good Dr. Watts' conception of the Hymn as the singer's devotional response to God's revelation of Himself—in Scripture indeed, and also beyond Scripture, through a living Christ and a personal experience, dominates the situation completely. And it seems to us to reveal and to deepen the true relation of our hymns to Scripture, because it is so obviously a reversion to the Pauline ideal of Christian song and so faithful to the spirit and the letter of such of the primitive hymns as have survived.

LECTURE THREE

THE RELATION OF THE HYMN TO LITERATURE

LECTURE THREE

THE RELATION OF THE HYMN TO LITERATURE

I. Leo X's Scheme of a Classical Hymnody

The relation of the hymn to Scripture was presented in the last lecture as a phase of the subject that has been in the mind of the Church from the beginning, often pressing heavily upon its conscience also.

The same thing cannot be said of the relation of the hymn to literature. The great poetry of the Psalms was the specific inheritance of the Christian Church; so also was that Hebraic tone of mind Matthew Arnold so greatly deplores as an impediment to true culture. And that mind was more alert to what the Psalmist called the beauty of holiness than what a modern poet has called the religiousness of beauty. That some of the early fathers were deeply conscious of the poetic elevation of the Psalms hardly needs saying.

It is likely that the church hymns, as distinguished from the Psalter, were not very definitely subjected to what we would mean by literary criticism until after the spirit of humanism had taken possession of Papal Rome. When the classical Revival was at its height Leo X (1513-21) was minded that the daily offices of the Church should find a new expression in a "Latin more pure, more spirited, more elegant." He began the revision of the Breviary by committing its hymns to an accomplished Latinist, Zacharias Ferreri, for rewriting. And he in 1525 printed his new and classical hymnal with the approbation of Leo's successor, Clement VII.

I cherish a copy of Ferreri's hymnal,[1] sumptuously bound as befits so elegant a specimen of typography, as an engaging and now innocuous memorial of the first concerted movement to ally church hymnody with literature. An intrusion of pagan mythology gave already a wrong turn to the movement, and yet the classical hymnal was not without its own felicities; as in this verse of the hymn on St. Francis:

"Far in the greenwood's shadow and its silence
Lonely he walked, while Heaven itself grew nearer;
Pure were the thoughts that in his gentle bosom
Rose and were cherished."

II. Calvin's Poetical Standard of Psalmody

Calvin's distaste for the elaborated art of the Roman ritual has hidden from friend and critic alike his zeal for such beauty as was compatible with his simpler standards of worship.

Excepting Leo, he is the first church leader who deliberately set up a literary standard for his church song and called a poet to his service. But the Pope kept within church circles and committed his project to one of his bishops. Calvin went farther afield. In a time of bitter controversy he ignored all party affiliations and chose as the poet of Reformed Psalmody Clement Marot, a reformer only to the extent of favoring a house cleaning, and with whose manner of life Calvin could have no sympathy. But a poet,—a maker of ballads, rondeaux, love songs, society verse and court poetry; graceful, debonair, light-hearted, sometimes hiding real feeling beneath trifling, sometimes revealing it in serious verse that charmed his generation. The last man in France, one would say, to attract Calvin, yet to his mind the only man in France to clothe his new psalmody with the grace he craved.

It is easy to say that Calvin's scheme of a version of the Psalms put into current French meters, that people might sing them, was in itself a sin against literature. And that may be true. But it was Marot the poet, not Calvin the reformer, who first conceived the scheme. Fluttering around the court, ambitious to be court-poet, Marot began versifying Psalms in the meters of popular songs, handed them around among the ladies and gentlemen of the court, and with the Dauphin's aid got them sung.

When Calvin made his little psalm book of 1539 at Strasburg, twelve of these court-songs had come into his hands. He appropriated them all, and added a few of his own making. Marot's work became his standard, his own a temporary makeshift; discarded as Marot began to print more versions.

Marot's Psalms got him into trouble. The Sorbonne thought they infringed the Theological Faculty's monopoly in interpreting Scripture. And under the leadings of providence, as strange as it is kind, Marot came to Calvin's very side at Geneva as an exile.

The sight of the great congregation in the cathedral and the volume of united voices praising God in their own tongue seem to have moved many travelers. It was all a novelty. It moved Marot most of all, for the French Psalms they were singing were his own.

He was easily persuaded to go ahead with his versifying, and Calvin was keen for a complete Psalter. I like to think of the ardent reformer and the debonair poet side by side in Genevan streets.

Marot added twenty Psalms to the poetic stock. Calvin urged the Council to make a grant that would induce the poet to carry on. They declined, whether from parsimony or from annoyance at the poet's refusal to wear the yoke of Genevan discipline. Calvin did nothing toward completing his Psalter as long as hope remained of completing it on Marot's level. It was not till after Marot's death that he entrusted it to Theodore Beza.

III. English Psalmody Apart from Literature

The Psalms of Marot crossed the Channel in the active give and take between the courts of Francis I and Henry VIII. And one might say that they crossed in two separate parcels.

To the rising school of poets at the English court they represented the work of a distinguished writer and a new sort of court poetry. They suggested the Psalms as a mine of poetic material. They started a fashion of versifying them. The Psalms of Surrey and Wyatt were literary exercises of this sort. They had no bearing upon an English ordinance of Psalmody.

There was, however, at Henry's court, a groom of the chambers, Thomas Sternhold, to whom the French Psalms represented a Reformation movement to provide the people with religious songs in their own tongue. He felt a call to emulate Marot by turning some Psalms into the English ballad meter, in the hope of replacing the amorous songs popular at court.

These simple versions of Sternhold, as the Reformation gathered way, proved to be the nucleus of the metrical Psalter which in Elizabeth's time became the congregational praise book of the English Church.[2]

Its Psalms throughout follow Sternhold's model. They are mechanical verse; sometimes doggerel bearing the same relation to literature that the lines above Shakespeare's bones bear to Shakespeare's plays. Only one exceptional passage survives in the poetic anthologies:

"The Lord descended from above,
and bowed the heavens hie:
And underneath his fete he cast,
the darkness of the skye.
On Cherubs and on Cherubins,
full royally he rode:
And on the wings of all the windes
came fliying all abrode."

These *Sternhold and Hopkins* Psalms played a brave part while the Reformation glow lasted; and well into the nineteenth century they continued dear to the rustic mind, which likes its poetry plain. They never could have satisfied a sensitive taste, and, as their use lingered, they caused chagrin and aroused ineffective hopes for something better.

In that light we are to set the seventeenth-century Psalm versions of such writers as Bacon and Milton. They were not offered as poems but as samples of a betterment of the current psalmody on lines that might prove feasible. You could hardly expect a generation brought up on Martin Tupper to pass at once to Robert Browning. It was so, I fancy, that these proponents of new versions argued. None certainly, unless the Sidneys and Sandys, achieved anything resembling a poetic Psalter.

Nor could that be claimed for Tate and Brady's *New Version*,[3] which at the beginning of the eighteenth century won its way into London and beyond, and in time became the classic psalm book of Massachusetts Arianism. Unjustly ridiculed, it was a great advance over the *Old Version*, in the flowing rhythms that make for singing and the happy phrasing that makes for poetry even though falling short of it. How many hymns have a better opening than "As pants the hart for cooling streams" and "With glory clad, with strength arrayed"?

There is less to be said for the new *Psalms in meeter* [4] adopted by the Scottish Church in Westminster Assembly days. The manner of its rescension, line by line, in open meeting, the sacrifice of all beside to "purity," remove it altogether from the sphere of letters; just as the inweaving of its strains into the fabric of Scottish piety remove it from the sphere of mere criticism. It was the romance of these tender associations, no doubt, that made Sir Walter Scott so hostile to any improvement of Scottish psalmody.

But indeed the whole vast body of English Psalm versions hardly relates itself to literature at all, as we define literature now. It is a transcription of Hebrew poetry on a great scale, in which conscience rather than taste presided over the long process of journey-work.

IV. Religious Lyrics and the First English Hymn Book

As long as Psalm singing was the established order in every English parish church, there was no motive for writing congregational hymns. But not even proscription can quite seal the fountains of holy-song. As early as the times of Elizabeth and James, when the practice of music was common, there were sacred lyrics, adapted for part singing to the accompaniment of lute or viol.

Of Thomas Campion's *Two Bookes of Ayres* (c. 1613) the first is given over to "Pure Hymnes such as the Seventh Day loves": spiritual and poetic enough to tantalize the editors of modern hymnals. Josiah Conder adopted "Never weather-beaten sail more willing bent to shore." If we need more hymns of the heavenly homesickness none is lovelier. More lately *The Oxford Hymn Book* has included his "View me, Lord, a work of Thine." These bring Campion into an actual connection with the origins of our English hymnody as unique as it is unrecognized.

Campion was not consciously composing congregational hymns. There was just one way of getting such into parochial worship at that date, and that was the application of force. It was soon applied by an ambitious poet, George Wither, in one of those eruptions from beneath the commonplace surface of things that upset the natural order of events.

After some years of quiet preparation Wither amazed the Church and challenged the book interests by printing in 1623 his *Hymnes and Songs of the Church*, fortified by an order from King James that the Company of Stationers should bind it in with every copy they issued of the Metrical Psalter. The English Church, that is to say, was to start singing hymns under civil compulsion, and the hymns to be sung were Wither's. His personal poverty afforded the occasion; his high appreciation of his own work was his apology.

But his work is as hard to account for as his temerity. The only trace of his earlier lyrical charm is in some unwanted love-songs from *The Song of Solomon:*

"Come, kiss me with those lips of thine;
For better are thy loves than wine;
　And as thy powered ointments be,
Such is the savour of thy name.
And for the sweetness of the same,
　The virgins are in love with thee."

The body of the book is hardly more than doggerel, dull with platitude and piosity.

The hymns in his *Hallelujah* were written after he had given up his hopes of enriching church worship, and were designed to hallow private life. Aiming to cover every act and occasion, they burden each one by appending a string of moralizings. "A Hymn whilst we are washing" forbids us to regard even so simple a duty as its own reward. Two or three of better type have been revived lately,—"Come, oh come, with pious lays," and "Behold the sun that seem'd but now." There is no doubt that Wither aimed at allying hymnody and *poetry;* for in the preface he calls himself a successor of George Herbert in "turning his muse to divine strains."

The *Hymnes and Songs of the Church* still holds

our interest; because if the Company of Stationers had not gone to law, it would have been the first hymn book of Protestant England.

It is interesting to speculate on what might have happened if Wither's zeal had been less egotistical; if he had sought to enlist the services of the remarkable group of devotional poets who illuminated the evil times of Charles I. Supplying the motive, what a hymn book they could have made—Quarles, Herrick, Herbert, Crashaw, Traherne, and, later, Vaughan!

Only Quarles had the public ear. Herrick's litany shows that he could write hymns. George Herbert's lyrics of pure devotion, which he loved to sing alone, would have been less eccentric in form if many other voices were waiting to join in them. Crashaw's emotion and lyrical gift needed the restraint that hymnody imposes. Traherne tried an apprentice's hand at hymn making. And Vaughan really worked out alone the conception and form of congregational song in such lyrics as:

> "My soul, there is a countrie:"
> "Up to those bright and glorious hills."

They are beautiful and still available. With little relation to the church hymnody that was to be, they are very suggestive of the church hymnody that might have been.

As things were, the figure of George Wither

stands alone, three-quarters of a century ahead of his time; an interesting and pathetic adventurer, an ineffective leader.

Even so we must grant him the third place in the succession of those who have striven for a poetical hymnody: Leo, Calvin, Wither.

V. The Poetic Hymnody of the Restoration

During the Puritan ascendancy, which Wither lived to see, all the zeal was for psalmody; and Parliament mingled piety and politics in futile debatings whether Rous' or Barton's version was "purer."

Not till after the Restoration of 1660 the wind began to change; and it brought a feeling of hymns in the air. In Jeremy Taylor, inside the Church, and John Austin, who had left it, the feeling took shape in an effort to revive the Office hymnody. There were also a number (hardly a group) of men who felt more freshness in the air and the prophecy of a more modern hymnody.

Bishop Ken's morning, noon and evening hymns also carry a reminiscence of the daily Office, but humanize it with a vitality that has defied criticism. The melodious hymns of Samuel Crossman, "My song is love unknown," "My life's a Shade, my daies," are inventoried by Matthew Arnold among his "awful examples." His objection is to the choppy "Hallelujah meter." But, when a writer turns a trying meter into melody, the criticism seems invalid. Richard Baxter's "Lord, it belongs not to my care" is included in Palgrave's *Treasury of Sacred Song*. As are four of John Austin's and three of John Mason's. There is the witchery of competent verse in Mason's:

"My Lord, my Love, was crucified;
He all the pains did bear;
But in the sweetness of His rest
He makes His servants share."

So gather at our call a number of writers of the late seventeenth century, the predecessors of Isaac Watts. By no means the equals of the Caroline group, yet their work responds to the reasonable demands of Christian culture, and at its best rises into poetry. It was, however, destined to be overlooked in a movement for a more popular type of hymn about to begin.

VI. Watts' Divorce of Hymnody from Literature

These Restoration singers had neither the muscles nor the tools to make a breach in the solid bulk of the old psalmody. They left it to Isaac Watts to say what English hymns ought to be and to furnish them. We have studied his performance in its relation to the Scriptures, and must now put it into relation with literature.

For a century and more Watts held a supreme place in the worship and the imaginations of Nonconformists. They cherished a conception of his place among poets possible only to a very provincial point of view. Or one would think so. But one's eyes open to find so late as September, 1858, *The Christian Examiner*, representative of Boston culture, gravely affirming that "Watts falls below Shakespeare and Milton in sublimity of thought."

In recent criticism Watts hardly figures at all. Dr. Schelling brushes him aside from the path of *The English Lyric*. He finds no place in Palgrave's *Golden Treasury*, but elsewhere its editor counts him "one of those whose sacrifice of Art to direct usefulness have probably lost them those honors in literature to which they were entitled."

That is very much Watts' judgment of himself. He thought himself a poet, and the reception accorded his *Horæ Lyricæ* (1705) confirmed his judgment. In later life he came to feel that his *Psalms and Hymns* were the greatest things he had done. He did not regard them as poetry but as the evidence of his renunciation of poetry for edification's sake.

To explain Watts and to justify his method we must recall the audience he addressed. Independency had only lately won through persecution and suffering and had not yet attained social respectability. The people who held on were mostly humble souls of dogged loyalty and narrow convictions. And for them Watts wrote his hymns. He kept his eye, while writing, not on the exceptions or even the average level, but rather on what we might call the underworld of Nonconformity,—"vulgar Christians" he called them, and "the meanest of 'em."

Dean Farrar, once asked how he managed to preach at Windsor to a congregation ranging from the royal family to the scullery maids, replied, "I prepare my sermon for the scullery maids, so that I can be sure the Queen will understand it." Watts prepared his hymns for "the scullery maids," but with even less thoughts for a Sir John Hartopp or Lady Abney of dissent.

These are phrases from the original preface:

[I have] "endeavored to make the sense plain and obvious."

"The metaphors are generally sunk to the level of vulgar capacities."

"Some of the beauties of Poesy are neglected, and some willfully defaced."

"I have cut out the lines that are too sonorous . . . lest a more exalted Turn of Thought or Language should darken or disturb the Devotion of the plainest Souls."

He goes on to explain that he had excluded such hymns as were more figurative or more ambitious, and would reserve them for the next edition of his "Poems."

The sum of it all is that the man who stood at the fountain-head of English hymnody chose to open a spring outside the area which we call literature, and arranged a water-course for its outflow in the direction in which the two streams, poetry and hymnody, were least likely to meet and coalesce.

His motive (covering both his "Psalms" and hymns) was to furnish an evangelical church song. His method was to find the quickest available descent to the level of the humblest Christian.

One poetical result that method did achieve, however unintended. It relieved the hymns of a great deal of poetical baggage: those high-flying rockets of imagery, that opulence of artificial adornments, which were at that time regarded as essential to poetry, but which are so repulsive to us. Apart from that Watts' method produced a body of virile verse that stated and applied the gospel to the various experiences of life very lucidly and so sympathetically that myriads of people learned to use his hymns as the natural expression of their own religious feelings.

In that fact lies the justification of Watts' method; and it brought about the complete and final vindication of the hymn of human composure in English-speaking lands. And thus the whole body of Watts' work earns a place in the literature of power; the literature that leaves esthetic critics cold while it moves men.

The body of his work now lies far behind, and there is none to suggest its revival. But however hardly Watts tried to suppress his poetic feeling, it was *a priori* unlikely that his work should never rise above the level of his accommodated verse. In some hymns the poet seems to throw aside the preacher's gown, to become unaware of the meanest Christian, to walk with God on higher ground. And these, unless we care to pose as meanest Christians still, are the songs by which Watts should be remembered, and which we may be glad to sing:

"When I survey the wondrous cross:"
"Our God, our Help in ages past:"
"There is a land of pure delight:"
"My God, how endless is Thy love:"
"Hush, my dear, lie still and slumber."

It is the fate of a man who succeeds conspicuously, especially of a pioneer, to set a fashion and furnish a model. Watts made the model for English hymns just as Ambrose did for Latin. And as Ambrose's were succeeded by the "Ambrosiani," so Watts founded a "school" of writers, procreated by his vitality and inspired by his facility. Dr. Doddridge was head scholar and Anne Steele a good second. Indeed her truly feminine emotionalism for a time deceived the elect into believing she was founding a school of her own.

A long train of writers followed, happily for us not needing to be catalogued in a survey of the relation of hymns to letters. You cannot get a sense of their number, and of their skill in reproducing Watts' faults, from any book on Hymnology. You have to be a grim collector of their eighteenth century hymn books to understand how diligently they debased the current coinage of the kingdom with alloy much less costly to the coiner than poetry is, though of course without any thought of counterfeiting.

VII. The Wesleyan Hymns as Poetry

The Wesleys were the first to contest the unliterary standard of the hymn Watts had set up.

The brothers had been reared in the very atmosphere of poetry. The love of it and the divine afflatus itself moved a number of Samuel Wesley's household; surely the most interesting family of modern England, till we come to the Rossettis and Archbishop Benson's.

Charles Wesley began writing hymns at once upon his conversion, and, one may say, wrote them spontaneously until his death. We have John's assurance that his own part in the vast bulk of the Wesleyan hymnody was small. The translations from the German are certainly his, and remain the best ever made. They are so little appreciated that it is pleasant to remember that his "Thou hidden love of God, whose height" was the prime favorite of so high a soul as Emerson: to hear that gentle voice chiding Moncure Conway, after service in his London chapel, for omitting even one verse of it.

But the whole body of the Wesleyan hymnody may fairly be regarded as a joint enterprise. It was John who conceived the ideal of a Methodist poetry, who appointed his brother poet laureate of the

Movement; who stood behind him as patron and beside him as redactor, and who superintended the printing.

The hymns were a part of Wesley's scheme of education. Behind the long succession of "Hymns and Sacred Poems," hymn books, and the cheaper hymn-tracts that followed almost with the regularity of a periodical,—behind them all was the single purpose of elevating the humble minds of his followers by the inspirations of poetry, and the unfailing conviction that in his brother's verse he had found the medium. The fullest expression of that purpose and conviction is the preface of the final Methodist Hymn Book of 1780; the largest collection he made of his brother's hymns:

"May I be permitted to add a few words with regard to the poetry? Then I will speak to those who are judges thereof, with all freedom and unreserve. To these I may say, without offense. 1. In these Hymns there is no doggerel, no botches, nothing put in to patch up the rhyme, no feeble expletives. 2. Here is nothing turgid or bombast, on the one hand, nor low and creeping on the other. . . . 4. Here are (allow me to say) both the purity, the strength and the elegance of the ENGLISH language: and at the same time the utmost simplicity and plainness, suited to every capacity. Lastly, I desire men of taste to judge (these are the only competent judges) whether there is not in some of the following verses, the true Spirit of Poetry; such as cannot be acquired by art and labour; but must be the gift of nature. By labour a man may become a tolerable imitator of SPENSER, SHAKESPEAR, or MILTON, and may heap together pretty compound epithets, as PALE-EYED, WEAK-EYED, and the like. But unless he is born a Poet, he will never attain the genuine SPIRIT OF POETRY. . . .

"When poetry thus keeps its place, as the handmaid of piety, it shall attain not a poor perishable wreath, but a crown that fadeth not away."

This is John Wesley's characteristically complacent stand in the matter of the relation of the hymn to literature. He takes his place as fourth in the line of church leaders who have sought to ally hymnody with poetry: Leo X, Calvin, Wither, Wesley.

Was Wesley justified in regarding his brother's hymns as poetry?

There is nothing conclusive in a suggestion that his judgment of poetry was capable of being warped by the pull of affection; as illustrated by his tribute to John Byrom's verse. It is more to the point to ask if his judgment of his brother's work did not in fact show a rather keen appreciation of just where the springs of poetry are to be found and as to what effects in us it is fitted to produce.

If we apply to Charles Wesley's hymns the tests of poetry in Mr. John Drinkwater's sane and pleasant book, *The Muse in Council*,[5] we can hardly fail to become aware of an unanticipated area of coincidence.

The essential thing behind poetry, Mr. Drinkwater tells us, its occasion as well as its spring, is "a most vital and personal experience." The things "characteristic of fine poetry can be achieved by intense individual experience and from no other source whatever." So far certainly Charles Wesley does not fail us. He had within him the springs of poetry in experiences as deep, as vital, as overwhelming, as man's can be. His hymns spring from discoveries of great truths passionately appropriated through a great experience working through feeling and passing into the imagination.

Now "it is of the necessity that such experience finds, when it is most profound, to state itself in perfectly selected and ordered words," that poetry comes into being. And its second test lies in the power of the poet's "pregnant and living words" "to compel in us an ecstasy which is exactly a response to that ecstasy of his own." It is questionable if any body of English verse ever met that test so fully as Wesley's did. It was the hymns of Charles and not the sermons of John that reproduced in thousands of lives the deep experiences of the poet. They created a new type of spiritual experience (and we still call it Wesleyan) that clothed the whole man with a mental and emotional mood, exalted, affectionate, ecstatic, tinged by mystical suggestion, lit by an aroused imagination. They imparted the touch of poetry to humble experiences.

I am far from accusing Mr. Drinkwater of saying that Charles Wesley was a true poet. I am only applying or perhaps misapplying his canons of poetry to a candidate of my own selection. In any case they can apply only to a small proportion of the vast production (some 6,000 hymns). That is all his brother claims for the selections he made,—that the body of it is good verse and that some of it exhibits "the true Spirit of Poetry." That fatal gift of facility led our poet precisely where it has led his betters in the poetic world, into a low country. And yet the surplusage conveys to me at least an implication of being written by a poet. Here is a copy of the 1780 hymn book. I open it at random at page 146, to an unregarded hymn (No. 143). And this is what catches my eye first:

> "Give me to bow with Thee my head,
> And sink into Thy silent grave;
> To rest among Thy quiet dead:
> 'Till Thou display Thy power to save:
> Thy resurrection's power exert,
> And rise triumphant in my heart."

Was it not written by an artist's hand?

The time-spirit is dealing more kindly with the Wesleyan hymns than with Watts? The Church at large cherishes a considerable group of them among her spiritual resources:

"Hark! how all the welkin rings:"
"Love Divine, all loves excelling:"
"Christ, whose glory fills the sky:"
"Come, let us join our friends above:"
"Come, Thou long-expected Jesus:"
"All praise to Him who dwells in bliss:"
"Christ the Lord is risen to-day."

Any one might serve to justify Wesley's estimate of his brother's gift. But the fact that all of them are still acceptable in use does more. It contributes something toward testing the permanent value of his proposed alliance of hymnody with poetry.

But I should like to test Wesley's ideal by a single example he would regard as too extreme; by a lyric of his brother's he would not admit into his hymn book. His reason is not far to seek. It lies exposed in the opening lines:

"Jesu, Lover of my soul,
Let me to Thy bosom fly."

Wesley's early experiences among Moravians, whose hymnody fell into a fleshliness altogether abhorrent, left a great repugnance to anything like fleshly imagery or terms of human endearment in prayer or song. The feeling is perfectly sound, and I share it to the full whenever I hear the popular "Safe in the arms of Jesus." But what Wesley perhaps failed to consider is that the fleshly image and the endearment are perfectly permissible in *poetry;* which, as Milton put it, should be not only "simple" (single in conception) and "passionate," but also "sensuous" (sensible) in its imagery. And that is precisely what happened in "Jesu, Lover of my soul."

It envelops us at once in the high atmosphere and transfiguring light of poetry, so that instinctively we lift the image and endearment to the height of spiritual exaltation, where the earthly love becomes the express image of the heavenly.

"Simple, sensuous, passionate." And what artistry! "The mere word-music," as Professor Saintsbury has said,[6] "is fingered throughout in the most absolutely adequate manner." The very opening word, "Jesu," is not "churchly," but marks a shrinking lest the hissing "s" mar the music.

Now we are dealing with the best-loved hymn in the language; the favorite of learned and illiterate, high and humble. And why is it so? No critic urged its acceptance. Average Christians could not analyze its appeal. Its tenderness is a part of that, but hundreds of the Wesleyan hymns are equally tender. Its spiritual reality is a partial explanation, but the hymns in general have as much. And after due tribute to these qualities the suspicion remains that the secret of its appeal lies in a poetic beauty that the average man feels without analyzing it, and in a perfection of craftsmanship that makes him want to *sing* it simply because it awakens the spirit of song in him rather than a mood of reflection.

From this single instance of an actual coincidence of poetry and popularity, there are no doubt a number of conclusions we might draw without straining ourselves.

There are two we have to draw:

1st. That poetic beauty in a hymn is not necessarily a bar to spiritual edification, even among humble people.

2nd. That the particular type of poetic beauty exhibited by the best loved hymn in the language is the lyrical type. The hymn is lyrical in the primary sense. It is a song and it evokes singing.

VIII. The Unpoetic Evangelical Hymnody

Charles Wesley's great lyric passed over to the Evangelical side of the Revival in Whitefield's hymn book, and also, strangely enough, in Toplady's. Toplady's book was a sincere effort to embody his prefatory statement that anything designed for worship should keep in view that God is not only "the God of *Truth*" but also "of *Elegance*." He had some gift and practice of poetry, and his "Rock of Ages" is the one hymn on the Evangelical side worthy to parallel "Jesu, Lover of my soul." "Elegance" was not the divine attribute that especially appealed to the Evangelical Revival or the Evangelical Movement that grew out of it.

The deep experiences and spiritual yearnings fostered by the Revival might very well have proved to be springs of poetry and were inevitably the occasion of much verse. Newton, Fawcett, Berridge, Cennick, Hart, Williams, Haweis, Peronnet,—these are some of the familiar names, not of poets but of authors of useful hymns fostered by the Revival. They were mostly humble people who wrote for their kind, occasionally rising to a height of emotional eloquence not untouched by imagination, as in Cennick's "Children of the heavenly King" and Williams' "Guide me, O Thou Great Jehovah."

Cowper was the poet of the Revival, but his share in its hymnody was accidental, a tribute to his friendship with John Newton. Many of his hymns are journey-work, produced at Newton's request, to follow his sermons. "Oh, for a closer walk with God" is a genuine lyric, because born of an intense experience and wrought into melody. It was the singular virility of Newton's contributions rather than the delicacy of Cowper's that made their *Olney Hymns* a classic manual of the Evangelical discipline.

There is, to say the least, a general feeling that the Evangelical point of view and the Evangelical handling of life tended to ignore "*Elegance*," to divorce rather than to cement culture and religion. The Wesleyan and Evangelical view-points met together in the spiritual intensity they invoked, but in their bearing upon the cultural aspects of life the advantage lay with the Wesleyan.

It was of course the Evangelical side of the Revival, rather than the Wesleyan, that became the great influence in determining the hymnody of Evangelical communions in America; both in forecasting its cultural relations and in furnishing its actual relations. It fixed, for instance, the basis of Presbyterian hymnody, when the extreme devotion to Watts had given away; a basis solid in piety rather than molded by art. If this Evangelical hymnody was not poetic, it did sound that note of holiness which Oliver Wendell Holmes, a liberal even among Unitarians, caught and which he missed from so many later productions.

The growth of general culture is now militating against the continued use of some of these eighteenth century hymns, precisely as in that century it militated against the continued use of the rude metrical Psalms. The progress of culture in the mass of the people is extremely slow, and is now in a backwater: but viewing humanity long-wise it is perceptible. And any movement to keep our hymnody abreast of it may be viewed complacently, for it is inevitable.

And thus the ground is laid for considering the last movement toward securing an alliance of hymnody with poetry.

IX. Montgomery's Critique of Current Hymnody (1823)

The accumulation of hymns, Wattsian, Wesleyan, Evangelical, awaited until 1823 the careful stocktaking by the poet James Montgomery in an essay prefixed to his *Christian Psalmist.*

"We have," he says, "hymns without number," but few "that lay claim to great literary merit."

Dr. Watts he characterizes as "one of the least of the poets of our country" but "the greatest name among hymn-writers," since "it pleased God to make his 'Divine Songs' a more abundant and universal blessing than the verses of any uninspired penman that ever lived." But the critic lamented much prosaic phrasing and those "rhymes worse than none" that encouraged the incompetent to imitate his faults.

Montgomery put Charles Wesley next to Watts; a man of genius with an affluence of diction and splendor of coloring rarely surpassed in treating Christian experience. His limitation is a "predilection to certain views of the gospel" that narrows his range. Addison's four hymns are "pleasing." But they neglect that celebration of God's grace which constitutes the glory of Doddridge, deficient as he often was in poetry and eloquence. Toplady "kindled his poetic torch at that of Wesley," but showed "a peculiarly ethereal spirit" of his own.

The school of Watts does not interest our critic.

He praises Cowper's poetry and Newton's virility. Among the outpourings of the general choir he finds not a few which "refute the slander that hymns are necessarily the least intellectual or poetical specimens of literature." "The God of Abram praise" is a noble ode. The short rescension of "Jerusalem, my happy home," "by an unknown hand" (often since attributed to the critic himself) is "delightful."

Montgomery was a facile poet in the narrative and descriptive manner, and was, Allibone tells us, "a favored guest at every fireside, and the companion alike of childhood and old age." These words grew pathetic to me as I threaded the thousand pages of his "Poems" to find a passage or a lyric worthy a place in even a liberal-hearted anthology. But by some instinct Montgomery understood the hymn better than most. Two or three of his own would be his best contribution to a poetic anthology:

> "Forever with the Lord:"
> "Prayer is the soul's sincere desire."

His estimate of what was then in stock was a fair appraisal. He finds a standing place for the hymn; that sometimes has been watered from the spring overflow of the stream of poetry on the one side, and never swamped by the wide waters of commonplace on the other.

X. The Lyrical Movement in Hymnody

This *Christian Psalmist* of Montgomery was an attempt to gather the best that had been done. Four years later, in 1827, two books appeared which looked forward rather than back, and caught the light of the newest movement in poetry which we are agreed to call the Romantic Revival. These were *The Christian Year* of John Keble and the *Hymns* of Bishop Heber.

The Christian Year, in its meditative way, brings the feasts, fasts and offices of the Church of England within the transfigured world of nature and life created by Wordsworth and Shelley and Keats; and views them through an atmosphere of romance. Keble was not thinking of church hymns. Those for morning and evening we have taken from his book, however effective, are merely extracts from his poems. But he furnished the point of view, the atmosphere, the manner, that make for poetry in many an English hymn.

The other book, the *Hymns* of Reginald Heber, still stands four-square against the background sketched by Montgomery. It was the memorial of an effort thwarted and yet so effective as to entitle Heber to a fifth place in the succession of church leaders who have sought to ally hymnody with poetry.

Early in life he had formed an estimate of the current hymns less favorable than Montgomery's. He then conceived the bold scheme of preparing a Church of England hymnal in which every number should be a lyrical poem. He sought his models and helpers in the current school of romantic poets. His affiliations were not with Wordsworth's philosophizing. They were with the group led by Walter Scott; with his sense of the picturesqueness of olden times, with the romance of adventure in Southey, with the ringing melodies of Campbell and Byron and Moore. He appealed to Scott, Southey, Milman, and other friends for contributions to his book, and to the bishops for its authorization. Most of the poets failed him and the bishops hesitated. The book was never printed by him.

After Heber's death John Murray brought out his *Hymns* in the wide-margined octavo bound in gray boards that was the recognized format of Byron and Murray's other poets. Inwardly its distinction lay in the fifty-seven contributions of Heber, already a venerated figure, and twelve of Henry Hart Milman, then at the height of his fame as a writer of poetic drama.

Everything about the manner of publication was intended to suggest poetry. It was a recommendation of hymnody to high and dry churchmen disposed to decry it and a challenge to London literary circles. It was a hymnody with the spirit, the free rhythms and ringing melodies of the new romantic poetry.

There were no precedents for such picturesque hymns as:

"Hosanna to the living Lord!"
"From Greenland's icy mountains:"
"The Son of God goes forth to war:"
"Brightest and best of the sons of the morning:"
"By cool Siloam's shady rill:"
"When through the torn sail the wild tempest is streaming."

Some of Milman's might have been songs from his dramas:

"The chariot! The chariot! its wheels roll on fire:"
"Ride on! ride on in majesty!"
"Bound upon the accursed tree:"
"When our heads are bowed with woe."

The point is not that these lyrics were more poetic than the Wesleyan but that they were more aggressively so: as if Wesley had aimed to bring the hymn into the domain of poetry, and Heber had aimed to bring current ideals of poetry into the domain of hymnody.

He effected no revolution in sacred song as Watts had done, but rather injected his ideals to work as leaven. What his book accomplished was through the incorporation of every one of his own and several of Milman's lyrics into current books of various communions. Once there their contrast with their more drab surroundings could hardly fail to raise the question whether it might not be well that this remainder of the hymnody should likewise be lyrical.

Heber's hymns acted as a precedent, an encouragement toward a change in the literary standard pretty generally. I think it is fair to say that they are back of the very recent movement appropriating lyric poems even when it involves more or less of departure from the traditional hymn-pattern. Thus the Scottish Presbyterians led the way in adopting Tennyson's "Sunset and evening star": the American Methodists in adopting Lanier's "Into the woods my Master went": the Students' Christian Movement in adopting William Blake's

> "And did those feet in ancient time
> Walk upon England's mountains green?"

Such widely separated instances of what is coming to look like a common lyrical impulse are the more interesting because not concerted. Probably they suggest the direction in which our rapidly changing hymnody is pointed. But even so it would be premature, certainly, to claim at the present time that the English hymn is literature. There are in fact several interests which are not concerned that it should be or are actively in opposition to literary ideals.

There are, first of all, the strong pull of use and wont in the case of an inherited hymnody which was not framed by literary motives, and the more tender appeals of personal associations with familiar words. It is, however, also true that those who gauge hymns by old associations are continuously passing away.

I recall the venerable senior of those engaged with *The Hymnal* of 1895 pleading with tears for the retention of certain hymns that the immense majority of the present-day generation never heard of.

A second disturbing force is the downward pull of a Sunday school hymnody not brought under educational ideals and discipline. It is left very largely under the leadership that can be procured most cheaply. As things stand the songs taught through the most impressible years not only fail to familiarize our children with great hymns, but actually cultivate a taste for things that are unworthy. As the children take their places in the church the tastes and habits that have really been thrust upon them protest against acquiring a different and more elevated standard of praise.

The undeniable liking of the American people for light and catchy music readily coöperates with these graduates of the Sunday school in bringing into the church the kindred examples of what are called evangelistic songs. It is quite true that the words set to these melodies are seldom more than a verbal accompaniment to the tunes themselves. Only for some special ineptitude or on some special occasion does anybody give much thought to them.

There was such an occasion when "Beautiful Isle of Somewhere" was announced as part of the official program for the funeral of a President of the United States. The same song was included in the order of exercises at a vast rally of Sunday school forces at

Trenton in 1911. The then Governor of New Jersey, who was to occupy President McKinley's chair, interrupted the harmony of that occasion by calling attention to the extreme silliness of the words, and uttering an indignant protest against the whole method of the Sunday school interests which made such inane sentimentalities not only possible but officially appointed.

This occasion was exceptional in the prominence it gave to the words of one of the current songs. But the words are fairly representative of the only hymnody in use among considerable sections of church people, and whose popularity makes it a disturbing force. Only those engaged in the practical work of making hymn books are in a position to know the pressure brought to bear upon them to lower the cultural standard of church song.

XI. The Hymn as Related to Poetry

Every man of letters loves *The Book of Psalms:* not one praises the Metrical Psalter: all view the modern hymnal in a spirit of criticism.

The precedent was set, when hymns as distinguished from Psalms were new, by the great Dr. Johnson; who viewed them with an extreme aversion, partly because they were new and partly because they were loved by dissenters.

The famous passage from his *Life of Waller* is

too long to quote. Its substance is that every attempt to animate devotion by poetry has failed. We get nothing but "pious verse," useful only to assist the memory and please the ear. This failure is inevitable because intercourse between the soul and God is in a region beyond the scope of poetry, which loses its luster and power when it tries to decorate something more excellent than itself. Experiences of repentance, faith, supplication, thanksgiving, demand an expression the simplest and most unadorned.

All this seems rather empty of meaning till it dawns on us that Johnson shared with his time a definition of poetry long since outgrown. He thinks of art as opposed to simplicity. He thinks of poetry as the art of treating a theme by way of amplifying it, of hanging decorations on it, of recommending it by pleasing figures. So long as that definition persisted, Dr. Johnson's huge shadow lay heavy on the hymns he detested and extended over the whole area of religious verse. To our modern notions the criticism has no value. As Dr. Schelling puts it,[7] "The lyrist may sing the raptures of a pure soul in communion with God, or the apples of Sodom that turn to dust and bitterness between the teeth of the lost sinner. . . . There can be no limits set to art."

The prevalent modern criticism is headed by the great name of Matthew Arnold. As an apostle of culture the subject was much in his mind. His feeling is expressed as definitely as anywhere in his *Literature and Dogma:*

"Hymns, such as I know them, are a sort of composition which I do not at all admire. . . . I regret their prevalence and popularity among us. Taking man in his totality and in the long run, bad music and bad poetry, to whatever good and useful purpose a man may often manage to turn them, are in themselves mischievous and deteriorating to him. Somewhere and somehow, and at some time or other, he has to pay a penalty and to suffer a loss for taking a delight in them."

Before brushing this aside why not note that Arnold is merely applying to the main body of our hymns very much the same words that most refined and thoughtful Christians are applying to current "evangelistic" songs.[8]

May we not go a little farther with our critic? Is it not true of some of our church hymns that they fail to fulfill their high mission simply because they are not "good poetry"? Poetry has a singular property not only to arouse our dull feelings but actually to reproduce in us something of the high experience of the poet himself. Are we not prudent in coveting such a creative gift for our hymns?

Why is it lacking so often, even from those written by poets? Coleridge said of some of his own work that it was not poetry but thoughts expressed in verse. Apply that distinction to our hymns: for example to those of William Cullen Bryant. Every conscientious editor of an American hymnal must have scanned the hymns which the first of our poets to win distinction thought it worth while to gather into a volume, printed twice. But he scans them to little purpose. Bryant himself has explained their motive and origin. The earlier were written at the solicitation of Miss Sedgwick, who wished the rising poet represented in a new hymn book. The later were furnished at the request of some friend or committee to give distinction to a corner-stone laying or ordination or installation or what not. They have no poetic experience behind them. They are simply "thoughts for the occasion" expressed in verse. And that is why they fail us.

The case is not very different with the hymns prepared with the express purpose of edifying us: with the homiletical verse of Watts or Davies, that in the end remains not poetry but sermons; or the hymns leading up to a moralizing conclusion, like the Sunday school stories we used to give the children. It is regrettable that pastors continue to make such large use of them, doubtless as mere "fillers" or to illustrate a sermon-theme. For these uninspired verses have hardly retained their old capacity for teaching and admonition. They do not penetrate the crust of spiritual apathy that is part of the price the average Christian pays for sharing the complications of modern life. They do not arouse the congregation to spiritual idealism and holy imaginings. They do not light a candle in the modern heart.

Now, if these things are true:

(a) If Johnson's dictum that hymns are *theoretically* outside the sphere of poetry is unwarranted;

(b) If Arnold's criticism that our hymns are *in fact* outside the sphere of poetry is wholly justified in respect of the "evangelistic" hymnody and to a certain extent in the church hymnody;

(c) If there are certain properties of poetry that make it capable of adding something to spiritual beauty and encouraging spiritual vigor;

(d) If the Wesleyan hymns have demonstrated that the lyrical type of poetic beauty has the particular appeal to Christian feeling that awakens the spirit of song;

Then we seem to find solid ground for a conviction that the present-day lyrical impulse that is affecting our church hymnody is turned at all events in the right direction; that in following it we are really seeking the old trail which Calvin opened and which the Wesleys extended.

The lyrical movement no doubt has its own hazard, and it has two very definite limitations.

The hazard is implicit in the very motive of hymn singing; the heightening of religious emotion. The danger is of mistaking sugary sentiment for true feeling and its rhetorical expression in "soft luxurious flow" for true poetry.

The limitations of the movement are those suggested once for all by St. Paul, the first critic of Christian hymns and obviously the patron saint of this lectureship. "I will sing," he says, "with the Spirit": thus defining hymnody for always as a spiritual function. The Christian hymn, that is to say, even though it force a passage through the needle's eye of literary criticism, must always stand apart from the poetry that is dominated by purely esthetic ideals. It must compass spiritual beauty first of all: happy if, seeking the Kingdom of God first, His gift of poetry shall be added to it.

The other limitation St. Paul expressed by saying, "I will sing with the understanding also." For, if the spiritual function of hymnody is to extend into a social function, the hymns must be kept within the understanding of those who do the singing. Simplicity is not only a tradition but a principle of congregational hymnody. It does not follow that church songs should be so commonplace and obvious that the inattentive man, though a fool, need not err therein. It is better if they teach something we had not thought about or admonish us of something we had forgotten in life's rush.

At the worst St. Paul offers the alternate of "an interpretation." It is enough if there be an interpreter in the pulpit, ready and patient to disclose deeper meanings and hidden beauties beneath words that however simple are never as transparent as we suppose to an average Christian.

"A primrose by a river's brim
A yellow primrose [is] to him."

At the same time there is no place in popuiar hymnody for verse overweighted by philosophical thought, flamboyant with decoration, complicated by self-conscious ingenuity, or soaring to mystic heights that present no foothold for companionship. When such hymns occur in our books they are to be regarded as the indiscretions of an editor.

These two properties of the Christian lyric, spirituality and simplicity, are differential. They hedge the hymn not only from verse as a whole but even from the main body of religious verse. Each limitation will perhaps continue to act upon many of our poets as a deterrent and upon many of our critics as a taboo.

There is, however, no valid reason why poetry should not concern itself with the deepest feelings and highest aspirations of the spirit of man. There is no reason why hymn writing should not be recognized as a legitimate type of lyrical art. There is no reason why the poet's imagination and the poet's craftsmanship should not bring fresh offerings of strength and beauty into the sanctuary of God through the medium of the modern hymn as well as through the ancient Psalm.

LECTURE FOUR
THE CONTENTS OF THE HYMN

LECTURE FOUR

THE CONTENTS OF THE HYMN

The themes proper for a hymn, and the things it should contain or omit, depend altogether upon the theory we happen to hold of its function. And from the viewpoint of the various theories that have obtained our subject is best approached.

I. A Hymnody of Praise

And first the theory that *the hymn's special function is the praise of God.*

This was St. Augustine's, expressed in the first formal definition already quoted: 'Praise of God in song is called a hymn. It must be praise.'

The definition is still classical. Its echo is heard most clearly, oddly enough, in communions that are least liturgical. In them the hymnody is still "the service of praise." The long Psalmody Controversy was designated then and since as dealing with "the subject-matter of praise."

The practice of the Church never tallied with the theory. It accepted the Psalter, which contains much more than the praise-songs of Israel, but also enlarged it with songs of spiritual experience. The metrical hymns of Ambrose are more than praise.[1] Those who introduced varying "human composures" in the eighteenth century retained the Psalter for praise and appropriated the hymn to express evangelical convictions. The modern hymnal covers every type of religious expression, even the sigh of religious despondency, just as the Psalter did.

Nevertheless it remains true that reverence is the beginning of religion and gratitude the fount of Christian song; that St. Paul enclosed his "spiritual odes" in an atmosphere of thanksgiving; and that the hymn of praise is still the highest type of our church song.

Some recent hymnals, cumbered with many themes, tend to diminish songs of praise. The trend of their thought is away from a God above the world to a God immanent in the world and closer to life than breathing. The historic hymns that celebrate His infinite majesty lose spiritual reality to minds that pass through phases of mystical communion with God to what seems like coalescence.

Probably if all church song were praise, the praise would grow fulsome; certainly it would grow repetitious. Yet it has a high office all its own. Its loss would silence the leading note in the chord of devotion. Nothing but a "Sanctus" fitly anticipates those songs of the ransomed Church in *Revelation.* I have sometimes wondered whether it was his feeling for pure religion or his feeling for poetry that led Tennyson to regard Heber's "Holy! Holy! Holy! Lord God Almighty" as the greatest of English hymns.

II. A Hymnody of Edification

A second theory is that *the hymn's special function is the edification of the singers.* And so far as praise has a reaction of uplift the song of praise retains a place.

It is a theory that particularly commends itself to a generation much more keen for efficiency than worship. And it is quite certainly within the limits of St. Paul's charter. From this point of view the content of the hymn is:

1. An embodiment of some Christian truth; and hence the Doctrinal Hymn with its teaching power;
2. An embodiment of the spiritual interpretation of life; with its office of arousing spiritual feeling.

1. *The Doctrinal Hymn*

(a) The Doctrinal Mnemonic. In dealing with the disturbance at Colossæ, St. Paul put first the power of song to teach Christian truths. It would be hard to believe him so short-sighted as to neglect furnishing the Colossians with rhythmical formulas of things a Christian must know for his soul's health that could be set to familiar cantillations.

That is the doctrinal hymn in crudest form, the doctrinal mnemonic. When the Reformation came all the leaders except Zwingli put formulas of the faith into simple metrical forms. The once familiar tune "Commandments" is the melody to which Calvin set the Ten Commandments in his Genevan Psalter. And truly a wonderful thing is verse in its appeal to human instincts, in the power of its rhythmic march, its cadences and rhymes, to grip our minds and possess our memory.

We think of mnemonic hymns as bygone or as milk for babes. But there is no more perfect specimen than one in Cardinal Newman's *Dream of Gerontius*, which Dr. Sanday has included among the hymns for the University of Oxford. It begins:

"Firmly I believe and truly
 God is Three and God is One;
And I next acknowledge duly
 Manhood taken by the Son."

(b) The Didactic Hymn. It is a step upward from the mnemonic to the hymn that aims to convey doctrine didactically.

The most conspicuous modern advocate and producer of didactic hymns is Christopher Wordsworth, Bishop of Lincoln, in his *The Holy Year*, 1862. We have still with us several survivals of his "vehicles of sound doctrine";

"O day of rest and gladness;" tracing the origins and functions of the Christian Sunday:

"Holy, Holy, Holy Lord!"; a justification of the "Sanctus" and catalogue of the various groups of singers who employ it:

"O Lord of heaven and earth and sea;" which in

its full form enumerates the differing types of the divine gifts as the rationale and measure of our own.

None of these greatly warms the heart, but they are exceptional in being frankly didactic without quenching the spirit of song. For the weakness of didactic hymns is their didacticism. Our very nerves protest when we are asked to *sing*, and then rising find ourselves back in the school-room with a lesson in sound doctrine to be recited.

The success of *The Holy Year*, most likely, encouraged Samuel J. Stone, four years later, to undertake an explanation of the Apostles' Creed to the poor of his flock at Windsor in a series of hymns. The one now most familiar, "The Church's One Foundation," explains the article on "The Holy Catholic Church," and in method is rigidly didactic. Each line is a statement from the Bible, accumulated with an aim of justifying from Scripture the high Anglican doctrine of the Church; its divine authority, its sacraments, its essential unity, its communion of saints, etc. If this didactic method is what makes the hymn so effective among Christians of all types, then it is not only the peak of didactic hymnody, but distinctly a recommendation of didacticism.

My own impression would be that the hymn owes its power neither to its method nor its manner, but to an intense conviction and passionate loyalty written between the lines. As if a teacher were describing the features of his country to a class that were learning most of their geography from the thrill in their teacher's voice.

(c) The Doctrinal Lyric. And this forecasts the only type of doctrinal hymn which fully attains spiritual reality and whose teaching power far surpasses the formally didactic,—the hymn, that is to say, which presents doctrine lyrically, as mediated (I was about to say, filtered) through personal experience.

The special sphere of hymnody lies of course in the feelings rather than the understanding. The distinction between a catechism and a doctrinal hymnody is (or ought to be) that the first states doctrine with precision, the other in terms of feeling. The true hymn is conceived in feeling and aims to evoke it.

But then feeling, other than mere excitement, has its root in understanding. The hymn that cometh up like a flower and whose fragrance fills the sanctuary is always rooted in some doctrine; first apprehended and then transmuted through personal experience into a personal conviction. I believe, therefore have I spoken: but it is the feelings of the heart that make my words melodious.

A great hymn, I venture to think, is the fullest embodiment of Christian doctrine. For a great hymn is "the echo of a great soul" giving lyrical expression to truth apprehended through a high experience, in words that both use the common speech and transcend it.

This view would be confirmed, I am sure, by a review in chronological sequence of the hymn books of our English-speaking Protestantism. It was at the close of some such conspectus in a former Stone Lecture that the late Professor John De Witt wrote me:

"Really it awakens in me the suspicion that there is no better point of view from which to study the development and the reaches of Christian belief than that offered by hymnody. This is not strange, for after all beliefs of the first rate in influence receive, and, I have the impression, always have received their best and final embodiment in poetry, and especially in lyric poetry."

Poetry is not of course a suitable medium for the precise definitions that find place in a Confession. There is an illustration in Heber's great hymn. The opening, "Holy! Holy! Holy! Lord God Almighty" gives perfect poetical expression to the doctrine of the Trinity. The closing line, "God in Three Persons, blessed Trinity," instead of attaining a poetic climax, is not poetry at all but simply a reversion to Nicene definition. What poetry can do for doctrine is to humanize it, to set it in the light of imagination and to clothe it with feeling. And it is this handling of doctrine that has made the church hymn book the actual creed of countless thousands of Christians who have never so much as had the historic church confessions in their hands. I think this is still measurably true, though probably our hymns have never been sung so thoughtlessly as now, owing to that singular but prevalent gift of inattention so conspicuous just now in public worship.[3]

This gift of inattention, so far as hymnody is concerned, has been greatly fostered, no doubt, by the quick and rattling melodies and the rapid verse which the young people are trained to sing. In the meantime the teaching power of great hymns remains, an asset of the Church hardly included in the inventory of her educational resources, and in her educational practice generally disregarded. We ought, I think, to feel that the subordination of the hymn book to the catechism as a means of instruction is a Scottish inheritance rather than a counsel of prudence. Certainly it is opposed to the best pedagogy, and to a reasonable psychology.

In this place, at least, it ought to be sufficient to quote from the preface of Dr. Archibald Alexander's long-forgotten hymn book:[4]

"Evangelical hymns are peculiarly suited to be the vehicle of gospel truth to the young and ignorant. It is a fact that unlettered Christians retain in their minds more of the gospel in the words of the spiritual songs which they are accustomed to sing than in any other form, and children can perhaps be taught the truths of religion in this way, more effectually than in any other . . . the understanding is reached with most certainty through the feelings of the heart."

Dr. Alexander's words were printed a century ago, and it is quite possible that the Church's failure to act on them may bear some part in the net results of a Christian education that at a century's end has left the body of young people in what the chaplains of the Great War and the instructors in our colleges are agreed to call an astonishing ignorance of the very rudiments of Christian doctrine. I do not envy the man who may feel the call to conduct the rising generation through a course of systematic theology, addressed to minds so hostile to authority and so careless of discipline. But I do cherish a hope of reaching them, more insidiously, through the avenue of great Christian song that lifts us up from the levels of materialism almost in spite of ourselves to an atmosphere of spiritual feeling in which truth may be discerned.

2. *The Hymn of the Spiritual Life*

Christian doctrine lays the ground for a spiritual conception of life. And so the teaching hymn of St. Paul's injunction is coupled with the hymn of the spiritual life wherewith we "admonish one another." Those who interpret the phrase as "rebuking one another" travesty the whole subject and turn the fellowship of song into a scolding-bee. If we take the literal meaning of the Greek verb, "to put in mind of," then it complements "teaching" and fills out the twofold function of the Hymn of Edification:

1. To instruct us in the things we need to learn;

2. To bring to our remembrance the things that get crowded out of life: its atmosphere of grace, the heavenly call, the Christian ideals and sanctions, the incentives to brotherly service, the beauty of holiness, the hope of heaven,—in short, the spiritual conception of life.

These hymns of life fill the larger part in many of our hymnals. An editor's custom is to group them by subject, repentance, faith, love, hope, etc. But there are no partitions in the soul, where faith and love flow mingled through. The partitions of the hymn book are only a rough and ready attempt to classify by hand.[5]

We shall get at the contents of the hymns of life a bit more scientifically if we group them by their method.

(a) THE SERMONIC HYMN, whose method is homiletical. Very likely it includes doctrinal matter and almost certainly some exegesis, but it is sermonic because the value of its observations lies in the application of them. It is a sermonette in verse.

In the history of English hymnody the sermonic hymn was the first comer, the prototype. The large majority of Dr. Watts' hymns (I should think) are sermonic. Each carries its text as well as its theme at its head, and most of them proceed in the homiletic manner:

"Behold what wondrous grace!"
"Mistaken souls that dream of heaven:"
"Who hath believed Thy word:"
"Why should the children of a king:"
"How sad our state by nature is."

Homilies all, from text to application! Naturally so, because among the dissenters, for whom Watts wrote them, the homiletical ideal of worship dominated everything.

Inevitably so with the followers of Watts, who wrote their hymns under the sway of feeling aroused in composing a sermon; turning its points into verse for the very purpose of getting it sung at the sermon's close by the congregation who had heard it. The manuscript draft sufficed for the purpose, because the singing proceeded line by line as the precentor read it out.

All the hymns of Doddridge and President Davies of Princeton were made and used after this fashion, and not printed during their lives, unless the sermon itself happened to appear in pamphlet form.

The contents of the sermonic hymn are as wide as life:

The gospel hymn, "Not all the blood of beasts:"
The hymn of invitation, "Return, O wanderer, return:"
The call to repentance, "Deep in the dust before Thy throne:"

The hymn of confession, "Sin, like a venomous disease:"
The hymn of faith, "Faith is the brightest evidence:"
The hymn of consolation, "Why do we mourn departing friends:"
The call to battle, "Am I a soldier of the cross:"
The warning, "How short and hasty is our life:"
The last call, "Death! 'tis a melancholy day."

The sermonic hymn had a great day and to some extent survives. It is curious to note the revival of a rather pronounced homiletical method in the hymns of what is called the new social gospel. Our friends outside have caught not only the pulpit graces but even the pulpit twang.

(b) The Hymn of Personal Experience, which substitutes example for precept. The singer tells his own inward experience, his spiritual mood, his actual discoveries, his personal privileges. And these range all the way from the first joy at finding Christ in Bonar's exquisite "I heard the voice of Jesus say," through Charles Wesley's experience of temptation in "Jesu, Lover of my soul," to the heights of consecration in Matheson's "O Love that wilt not let me go."

These are known as the "I and my" hymns, in which the singer speaks for himself as against the "We" hymns, in which he strives to express the mind of the collective Church.

The particular object of marking this distinction is to clear the ground for a motion to exclude the

"I" hymns from public worship altogether. And the original proposer, or at least the first one with influence enough to make his motion heard, was Bishop Wordsworth in his *The Holy Year* we have already looked into. He supports it by two propositions:

(i) The impropriety, the egotism, the impertinence of any one person obtruding his personal feelings and experiences, and worst of all, his boast of special privileges, as a medium for the public prayer and praise of God's people.

I tried to show in the first lecture that St. Paul made individuality of the very essence of hymnody because it is a spiritual function, and only by singing one to another made into common song. If songs of the spiritual life are to have any part in our hymnody, what can they be except songs of some soul who wrote of what life meant to him? There is no other spiritual experience than individual experience; no songs that enshrine it that do not really begin with "I." It is personality, here as generally, that makes a lyric inspiring.

When the long-awaited *Presbyterian Hymnal* appeared in 1874, the editor had transposed Mrs. Steele's "Father, whate'er of earthly bliss" into a "We" hymn: "Give us a calm and thankful heart," and so on. The hymn was a favorite then, and the protest so immediate and so general that the publishers felt compelled to alter the stereotype plate.

(ii) The bishop's other ground for suppressing "I and my" hymns was their contrast to those of the early Church:—

"One of the most striking differences between Ancient and Modern Hymns is this,—that the former are always *objective*, the latter are very often *subjective*. The former are distinguished by self-forgetfulness, the latter by self-consciousness." And so on at some length; illustrating the offensive hymns not only by Watts' "When I can read my title clear," but by Wesley's "Jesu, Lover of my soul."

How often, one wonders, have the above words been quoted? In how many books incorporated? They lie before me, as I write, in the current number of a periodical cited by a Presbyterian clergyman as final evidence of the decadence of our hymnody.

But what ground of fact have they to stand on? The Psalms were the first hymns of the Church: the evangelical canticles perhaps next. Is the 51st Psalm purely objective? And would "The Lord is my Shepherd" be improved by remodeling into a "We" hymn? But, the bishop says, the "I" and "my" of the Psalms are "words of the Holy Spirit Himself speaking by a Prophet and King" collectively for the whole body of the faithful. If so, what the Spirit actually did was to inspire an individual to voice his personal trust, and then to set a precedent for the collective use of his "I and my" hymn. And the same thing must be said of Simeon's canticle, "Lord, now lettest Thou Thy servant depart in peace," which is not notably objective.

In the later hymns of the Latin Church,

> "Jesu, dulcis memoria,"
> "O Deus, ego amo Te,"
> "Adoro Te devote, latens Deitas,"

the bishop sees a decline from Catholicity, a tendency to individualism, an idiosyncrasy of Medievalism "anticipating the peculiar characteristics of Methodism."

The mere fact that such objections have been proposed and are somewhat widely held ought to serve not so much by putting the Church into an attitude of defense as by reminding her that the only way she can justify the admission of these lyrics of individual experience into her public song is by a somewhat anxious scrutiny of the lyrics themselves in the special interests of popular edification. Of any given hymn of Christian experience in public use it is not enough to say that the author was a saint, his experience a real one and his lyric a sincere record. It remains to inquire if his experience was edifying:—

(i) *There is the test of spiritual wholesomeness.* A study of the spiritual diaries of good people, such as Mrs. Burr has made,[6] reveals a morbid strain veining the experiences of elect souls, occasioned sometimes by bad health, sometimes by inherent weakness of the spiritual condition as revealed by contact with life. Such tendencies came to the surface certainly in the exciting atmosphere of the great Evangelical Revival of the eighteenth century, whose hymnody, so abundant and so spiritual, happens to be a main source of our own.

The spiritual writhings, the blackness of despair, the unfitness for life, which so many of the converts were called to pass through are somewhat appalling even in the reading. In the case of John Cennick it is only "delicacy" that forbears from regarding his state of mind as deranged. Happily this does not color his cheerful hymn, "Children of the heavenly King." But it does suggest a scrutiny of the large body of his hymnody. The poet Cowper, another convert, is the typical case of a beautiful soul struggling with congenital melancholia, spurred by the revival excitements at Olney into violent insanity. In reading his most touching hymn, "Oh, for a closer walk with God," I do not need to inquire how much is of grace and how much of melancholia, but I wonder sometimes if the promiscuous use of such tender regrets does really minister to the public health or only encourage private moods of spiritual depression.

We will all agree, I suppose, that the undoubted power these lyrics of personal experience have over us comes from their gift of suggestion, greatly augmented as it is by the witchery of rhythm and often by hallowed associations.

This being acknowledged, the Christian Church ought to be willing to listen at least to what the new Psychology has to say of this potent gift that lies in her hands to use to the best effect; and so far as she finds the ground firm and the air clear, she ought to apply its teachings to her own hymnody of edification.

I venture therefore to quote from Evelyn Underhill's *The Life of the Spirit and the Life of To-day:*

> "This tendency of the received suggestion to work its whole content for good or evil within the subconscious mind, shows the importance which we ought to attach to the tone of a religious service, and how close too many of our popular hymns are to what one might call psychological sin; stressing as they do a childish weakness and love of shelter and petting, a neurotic shrinking from full human life, a morbid preoccupation with failure and guilt. Such hymns make devitalizing suggestions, adverse to the health and energy of the spiritual life; and are all the more powerful because they are sung collectively and in rhythm, and are cast in an emotional mold."

Miss Underhill in a footnote goes on to apply her teachings to what she is unkind enough to call "Hymns of the Weary Willie type"; hymns of an experience that has grown tired and is disillusioned:

> "O Paradise! O Paradise!
> Who doth not crave for rest?"

(ii) *There is even a test of cheerfulness* by which our hymns may well be tried, notably the hymns of that Great Revival, but also, as a recent rereading convinces me, the evening hymns we sing as those shadows deepen that are so suggestive of the shadow of death.

The shadow of death lies very heavily on the hymnody of the Evangelical Revival. There hangs in my study an embroidered sampler dated 1788, in which "Ann Smith, aged 11," has lettered in various silks the text of Dr. Watts' "Hark! from the tombs a doleful sound." The piety that set such a task for childhood was an inheritance from the Revival in which Charles Wesley did not hesitate to offer the Methodists a hymn addressed to a corpse, "Ah! lovely appearance of death;" and a great number of Evangelical hymn writers felt called to follow up their themes until in the final verse they could consign them to the grave. There grew up a habit and then a tradition of thus shadowing the themes of life with life's inevitable goal. It is a tradition the Church has grown out of, and much of this depressing hymnody has disappeared in successive winnowings. But one is surprised, in examining our current hymn books, with the extent of the traces that remain; mostly, I suppose, because woven in with materials really edifying.

But the habit of living in the presence of impending death, so detrimental to bodily health, cannot be edifying to the spirit. As one matures in experience he realizes that the cheerfulness he always recognized as winsome is one of God's greatest spiritual gifts. Blest is any ministry which, to use Lord Balfour's words, "serves the great cause of cheering up." What ministry better adapted to that end than a cheerful Christian song? [7]

"Is any merry? let him sing Psalms" is St. James' little contribution to the apostolical ideal of Christian song; the wholesome Luther transposed, bidding us cultivate a merry mood while we are singing. Even yet the modern Church carries on the good tradition, as she recovers her spirits at Christmas time, and sings:

> "God rest you merry, gentlemen,
> Let nothing you dismay."

(iii) Of course *the supreme test of the fitness of a lyric of personal experience for congregational use is that of spiritual reality.* Eccentric experiences are entertaining but not edifying. Super-mystical flights perplex God's little ones. Temperamental attitudes are not imitable. Even the spiritual aspirations of a hymn must be kept at least within telescopic sight of the congregation.

We are not called upon to sympathize with a scrupulosity that demands from every one who joins in a common song the literal appropriation of its every phrase. That would make the singing of a hymn equivalent to signing an affidavit that all the facts and aspirations therein set forth have been verified in the singer's experience. But poetry does not come home to us in just that way. It helps us to reproduce the poet's experience by heightening our own. A lyrical hymn expresses a poet's experience higher than our own, let us say. He clothes it in words of beauty so that we may like it, and through liking may gain a longing for the heights. We may sing the hymn often before we learn to like it, and may like it long before we win the heights. But if it encourages a step upward it is a hymn of edification.

There are no doubt hymns which do formulate that affidavit for our use. Notably Dr. Watts' "Alas! and did my Saviour bleed," with its climax:

> "Here, Lord, I give myself away,
> 'Tis all that I can do."

But surely no prudent pastor would invite a promiscuous congregation thus to play the part of Ananias.

A congregation should be protected also, in the interests of spiritual reality, from an over-sentimentality in lyrics of personal feeling. Difficult as it may prove to draw the line, there is a real distinction between hymns that heighten religious emotion to good purpose and those that merely play upon undisciplined susceptibilities to the weakening rather than the strengthening of the will. For reasons that are well understood a too emotional devotion is apt to tend to an undue familiarity with the person of our Lord. A hymn whose words aim to transmute His spiritual presence into flesh and blood is certainly no nearer reality than the words of the priest performing the same function in the sacrifice of the Mass. The peculiarly feminine emotions of some of our hymns must seem very unreal to valiant souls.

There is even greater difficulty in applying the test of reality to the congregational use of the hymn of penitence. The outgoing Moderator of a recent General Assembly remarked in his sermon that "we have deleted sin from our hymn books." [8] Certainly any books to which the remark may apply have passed out of spiritual realities. The fact of sin is fundamental and is bound to color the songs of the Church till time ends. The question remains, how is our sense of individual sin best related to our hymnody?

In early New England it was regarded as sufficient punishment for the worst offense that it be confessed publicly before the Church. We will all agree, that if expediency demands that a great sinner "tell it to the Church," such public confession must be made in very plain prose. If no such expediency exists, I am disposed to feel that the cry of the soul from sin's depths may best be kept where none but God can hear. Or, if the need of confession be urgent, that it be made in confidence to one of God's ministers.

Reality demands of each one of us that we bring to God's house the burden of sinfulness. But that sense of sin creates no impulse whatever to sing. It is only the sense of sin forgiven that wakens the spirit of song. And I should say that our hymns should be confined to that phase of repentance which turns away from sin to behold the Lamb of God which taketh away the sins of the world. Is not that indicated by the fact that Monsell's "My sins, my sins, my Saviour" is so ineffectual in congregational use, while Miss Elliott's "Just as I am, without one plea" touches the common heart?

The menace of a public hymn of confession is the practical certainty that it will be taken upon many lips lightly. I have noticed that some who most favor their congregational employ are equally critical of "The General Confession" in the Prayer Book, on the ground that used promiscuously it is used with a thoughtlessness that breeds insincerity. But nothing applies to a formula of confession in very rhythmical prose that does not apply to a hymn of like content.

(c) THE HYMN OF PRAYER. In this third group of Hymns of Life, possibly only four familiar ones take prayer as a theme to be developed:

"My God, is any hour so sweet:"
"From every stormy wind that blows:"
"There is an eye that never sleeps:"
"Prayer is the soul's sincere desire."

The Hymn of Prayer is rather one in the form of prayer, with its petitions versified. Its contents cover life. No one can limit them except by abridging our desires. All we can demand is that the subject-matter be submitted to the same tests that determine edification in the hymns of experience.

The reason prayer occupies so small a place in a classified hymnal is because the whole book is so permeated by its spirit that segregation is impracticable. The doctrinal lyric, "Rock of Ages" is a prayer; so is the lyric of experience, "Jesu, Lover of my soul."

This preponderance of prayers is surprising only from the point of view claiming praise as the hymn's special function. For the "psalms" of the early Church were largely prayers, and in non-liturgical churches the hymn book has always been the people's prayer book. Its importance as such is greatly enhanced by the failure of our pulpit prayers to function as they once did. The ominous rubric, now so familiar in our orders of service, "*The congregation will remain seated during the prayers*," violates the law of probability. The probability being that a seated congregation is not praying, though possibly listening to the minister. As the 1787 draft of the Presbyterian *Directory for Worship* put it, "There cannot be devotion without the appearance of devotion." (This is not one of Chesterton's paradoxes, but a bit of sound psychology.)

Our hymns of prayer at all events are sung in an attitude of devotion and have the felicity of direct address to God. The rhythm of the verse that makes common utterance practicable, the glow of poetic feeling that reaches the heart, the medium of the music that helps to express the inexpressible,—all these features of the hymn of prayer enhance the opportunity it offers of real communion with God. And if it does no more than diffuse an atmosphere of reverence it has already brought an answer to its petitions.

The Metrical Litany is a special type of the Hymn of Prayer now familiar. Sometimes too much in the inventory manner, it is everywhere effective in "Father, hear Thy children's call," sung to Dr. Gower's music. By intention, no doubt, the metrical litany is a liturgical hymn, as in Pollock's sevenfold "Jesus, in Thy dying woes," designed to punctuate the seven-hour devotions of Good Friday. But "Just as I am" is also a litany, composed by a lady whose detestation of high church lacked nothing in emphasis.

Miss Elliott's hymn is in itself an ample vindication of the metrical litany. I have sometimes felt, as the address before the Communion closed with the words, "Let us therefore so come that we may find refreshing and rest unto our souls," and the congregation rises together to sing as an introit set to Barnby's music, that litany with its recurring refrain, "O Lamb of God, I come,"—I have sometimes felt that it was as perfect an expression of devotion as one is likely to come upon in this world.

III. A Churchly Hymnody

The third theory is that *the special function of the hymn is churchly.* It is distinctively church song, as being the authorized medium through which the congregation, as representing the corporate Church, can offer its praise in a way consistent with its unity and the appointed ordering of its worship.

That hymnody exists to supply the Church with hymns was obvious even to old-fashioned Presbyterians, as appears from the title of Dr. Charles S. Robinson's first book, *Songs of the Church.* And that the hymn fulfilled its function by contributing to public worship is implied in the title of his second, *Songs of the Sanctuary.* The theory that the hymn is church song in the sense of uttering the Church's voice is something quite different, and if applied to the contents of Dr. Robinson's books would much reduce their bulk.

The theory, as it affects English hymnody, is a product of the Oxford Revival of the eighteen thirties. It rests upon three foundations: a heightened conception of the Church, an ideal of worship as its corporate offering to God, and a new emphasis on the Church Year as the framework and calendar of that worship.

On these foundations the Oxford reformers proceeded to reconstruct English hymnody, partly by writing it anew, partly by shifting to the new basis so much of the old as it retained.

1. *The Hymn of the Church Militant*

The ideal of a corporate worship gives us first the Hymn of the Church, with its new note of self-consciousness, possibly of spiritual pride. The Church, as seen from Oxford, is portrayed, as we have discovered already, in a doctrinal hymn, "The Church's one Foundation." Quaintly enough the one that seems nearest to being its precursor did not come out of the Wesleys' high church period, but out of the heart of Connecticut Congregationalism,—President Dwight's "I love Thy kingdom, Lord." The only hymn on the Church that came out of the Evangelical Revival was Newton's "Glorious things of thee are spoken," with its Old Testament flavor and culmination of pure edification. Stone's typically Oxford hymn, "Round the sacred city gather," is also for edification, but how different the criteria of the Church:

"God the Spirit dwells within thee,
His Society divine,
His the living word thou keepest,
His thy Apostolic line.

"Ancient prayer and song liturgic,
Creeds that change not to the end,
As His gifts we have received them,
As His charge we will defend."

Such is the Church within the ramparts, and such when marching forth in Baring-Gould's "Onward, Christian soldiers" in martial parade, with the processional cross "going on before": like an army because corporate,—"All one body we."

The Oxford conception of churchliness, covering all life and endeavor, gives a new basis for the Hymn of Service also; making it distinctively a hymn of the Church militant; singing, while working the parish, of the Church's functions; singing, while working abroad, of the Church's commission.

And here, it seems to me, the sense of the Church's solidarity, the conviction that the call to personal service is within the one commission, the assurance that our work is included in the anticipation of the Church's victory,—these things make the hymn of service a new song by making it church song. The Christian who goes forth alone to solve the gigantic problems that face us, the evangelization of a reluctant world, the infusion of a spiritual conception of life into the social order, may steel his heart with the song of duty as he dips up the seas of human trouble with his little bucket, but I do not see how he can encourage his heart with the song of hope. It is the multitude of laborers that brings promise, the organization of labor that brings effectiveness. And if that be so the church song is the most inspiring hymn of service.

I am not sure that Oxford ideals have produced any very notable work-song, unless it be Bishop Coxe's "Lord, her watch Thy Church is keeping." What it has really done is expressed symbolically by the very simple act of gathering up all these hymns of varied service under the common heading of "Church Work."

At this point the Oxford Movement, which was ecclesiastical, is confronted by the recent Social Movement, which is secular. This makes a practical appeal to many of the least ecclesiastically-minded within the churches, who prefer to replace "the Songs of the Church" by "Hymns of the Kingdom," and who are no doubt one with us in heart and hope while they remind us that churchianity is hardly Christianity. They would generously coöperate with the great company of outside workers who turn their backs to the Church and sing ethical songs to church tunes. But it is a question how far there can be common song between church workers and those outside so long as the kingdom remains a spiritual kingdom, and its King is proclaimed Head of the Church. For how can two sing together unless they are agreed upon the key?

2. *The Hymn of the Church Triumphant*

The Oxford conception of the Church's continuity and solidarity did not fall short of heaven. It culminated there, and effected marked change in the contents of the songs of the heavenly home.

John Mason Neale's researches in medieval poetry and his brilliant renderings of some passages into English hymns grew out of a consuming desire to emphasize the historic continuity between the Latin and English churches. At the time the other-worldly type of religion inherited from the Evangelical Revival still obtained, and no part of his work appealed more than his group of New Jerusalem hymns:

> "Oh, what their joy and their glory must be:"
> Light's abode, celestial Salem:"

But more especially the three caught up so quickly from his version of the Rhythm of Bernard of Morlaix:

> "The world is very evil:"
> "Jerusalem the golden:"
> "For thee, O dear, dear country."

The "Jerusalem" motive was of course taken from Scriptures; but it was Scripture mediated through the Medieval Church. There was the same disillusionment in the then recent "I'm but a stranger here," as in "For thee, O dear, dear country." But the one was just a human sob: the other a voice from the cloister, shrining the monastic conception of life, the monk's rapt vision, his longing for release from this vile flesh; and so a part of the Church's unending song.

Even more expressive of Oxford ideals are the hymns that clothe heaven itself with a churchly fulfillment. They make us feel that the whole company of the faithful who have entered in are churchmen still:

"For all the saints who from their labors rest:"
"Hark! the sound of holy voices:
"Sing Alleluia forth in duteous praise:"
"Let our choir new anthems raise."

In these hymns "our departed friends" have merged into the "All-saints" of the liturgy. It is more than a change of manner, it is a sea-change, from Dr. Watts' vision of the individuality of "the saints above" in "Give me the wings of faith to rise" to these songs of the continuity and solidarity of a corporate Church whose unity is being fulfilled in heaven.

None the less not even the urge of an Oxford Movement can eliminate the personal equation. The stiffest churchman is only a vested man. And the editor of *Hymns ancient and modern* included his own "There is a blessed home." The contents of these personal hymns of heaven need as careful scrutiny as the more churchly. The complacent selfishness of Watts' "When I can read my title clear" has driven it from the hymnals. The unreality of the popular "Glory Song" ought to keep it from entering in. It blushes when it encounters Miss Rossetti's "Give me the lowest place."

3. *The Liturgical Hymn*

(a) THE HYMNODY OF THE CHURCH YEAR (*Hymni per totius anni*). Alongside of the Church Hymn the Oxford men established the Liturgical

Hymn: one whose contents are determined by the particular occasion of worship for which it is provided, and which occupies a definite place in the order of worship prescribed for that occasion.

It finds no special support, apart from his insistence upon eucharistic song, in St. Paul's injunctions, and does not need to. The Hallel of the Last Supper was a liturgical hymn in every sense and is a sufficient precedent. St. Paul was dealing with simple people gathered most unconventionally. Apart from some order for the Communion, a fixed ritual would have been as uncomfortable as we should find it at a cottage prayer meeting. Liturgies wait on architecture. In the course of time the stately basilica would no doubt suggest some reversion to old Temple ideals of worship. And so a liturgical hymnody is a development and not an inheritance from apostolic tradition or practice.

To our liturgiologists the pattern shown on the mount is not the worship of the Temple but that of the Latin Church as embodied mainly in the Missal or Mass-book and the Breviary or Daily Office book. Now in that model, the function of the hymn is purely liturgical; which is to say that each prescribed hymn is irremovably imbedded in some special Office appointed for some "Hour" of the day, some day of the week, or some season of the Church Year. No hymn but the one appointed can be sung at Prime and the one appointed for Prime cannot be sung at Matins, nor Tuesday's hymn on Sunday;

and so on through the year. And of course the content of the hymn is determined by the nature of the Office enclosing it.

In the English Reformation the Breviary was allowed to influence Morning and Evening Prayer, and the Missal to influence the Communion Office; but the Breviary hymns and the Sequences of the Mass dropped out altogether. When hymn singing was resumed in the Church of England it entered under the impulsion of the Evangelical Revival: it was distinctively an evangelical rather than a liturgical hymnody. The early Anglican hymn books made very little more recognition of the Church Year than did our Presbyterian *Psalms and Hymns* of the eighteen thirties and forties.

Gradually the feeling grew that the hymn book ought to be a companion to the Prayer Book, matching every date and occasion of the church offices with the "proper hymn." To accomplish this required a rearrangement of the church hymnal in which the main body of its contents would group themselves around the framework of the Church Year and offices of the Church. And this led naturally to the subordination or suppression of much familiar material not germane to the purpose, especially the evangelical hymn and the hymn of individual experience. In a spirit of conciliation rather than logically room was made in a sort of supplement for more or fewer favorite or desirable pieces under the heading of "General."

The filling out of this scheme called for much fresh material. There were no sacramental hymns in English charged with the high doctrine of the Oxford Revival; there was an insufficiency of materials for the greater festivals having just the right tone, and for many of the lesser occasions of the Prayer Book there were no hymns at all. The Latin hymns of the old Church, overlooked at the English Reformation and neglected since, now for the first time shone forth in their liturgical fitness and were translated by many hands. John Mason Neale even adapted some of the Greek Church hymns, and a growing company of writers produced fresh contributions to fill out the tale of a liturgical hymnody.

The new interest in Latin hymns, after encountering reproach, was to spread through Protestantism, and many of Neale's versions proved a permanent enrichment. As for more original contributions we must not forget that "Sun of my soul," "There is a green hill far away," "Art thou weary, art thou languid," "Lead, Kindly Light" (to name only a few), are as much a product of the Oxford Movement as are *Tracts for the Times* themselves.

And yet, what seems to an outsider an excessive devotion to liturgical ideals has diluted English hymnody, has weakened its hold on *men*, by introducing much material that illustrates the theory at the expense of the singers. *Hymns ancient and modern* was and is the prominent exemplar of high Anglican ideals. But what a superfluity of Latin hymns rendered in pedestrian verse! What forced tributes to an occasion or a saint! How can a sympathetic pastor give out such first lines as:

"Sweet flow'rets of the martyr band:"
"Why doth that impious Herod fear:"
"O sinner, for a little space:"
"Blessèd feasts of blessèd martyrs:"
"O Jesu, Thou the Virgin's crown:"
"Shall we not love Thee, Mother dear:"
"He sat to watch o'er customs paid."

One wonders how many of the incredible number of millions into whose hands *Hymns ancient and modern* has been put by their clergy join in rendering such strains, or whether a silent majority has not learned to take refuge behind the corporate theory of church song. And in gauging the contents of these new contributions we must think not only of what they offer but what they replace. For church hymnals have gained such proportions that room can be found for the new only by discarding so much of the old.

(b) THE HYMNODY OF THE CHURCH YEAR IN NON-LITURGICAL CHURCHES. They have been very slow to recognize even its greater days. The generation before mine could remember when New England Congregationalism frowned on any celebration of Christmas; when kindly parents wrestled with the spreading Santa Claus superstition by leaving quite empty the little stockings trustingly hung before the hearth. My own generation can recall when in Presbyterian churches Easter was recognized only by the absence on that day of many of the young people, seeking good cheer elsewhere.

The Westminster *Directory for the Publique Worship of God* had provided that "Festivall daies, vulgarly called Holy daies, having no warrant in the word of God, are not to be continued." The puritan tradition is what was to be continued. The fathers of American Presbyterianism struck out this taboo from their new *Directory for Worship*, leaving its pastors and parishes quite free in this matter, as they still are. The clergy were to prove much slower than the laity in exercising this freedom.

In the absence of leadership by the clergy, it has really been the laity, acting on sentiment, who have dealt with the Church Year in non-liturgical communions. The rigidity of the liturgical system and the filling up of the calendar with numerous occasions has not appealed to them. The saints' days, unless it be the touching All-Saints' Day, are likely to remain in sole possession of those with Roman or Anglican traditions. The typical American will leave his business to celebrate Washington's Birthday (regretting it does not fall within the football season), but he will not leave it for a service commemorating any of the saints.

The only parts of the Church Year that touch the common heart are its recognition of Sunday as the day of Christian worship and the days or seasons that commemorate the outstanding events of our

Lord's life. To that extent the Oxford influence has affected the church worship. And most of the hymnals of non-liturgical churches open with an adequate provision conveniently arranged, whether its sections bear such labels as "Nativity" and "Resurrection" or as "Christmas" and "Easter"; their intent being so obviously liturgical.

Of such a service-book the *Hymns for the Day* are the natural opening.

The Morning Hymn, to be effectual, should catch the sunlight on the world, and waken our better part to dedicate a new day:

> "Awake, my soul, and with the sun:"
> "As the sun doth daily rise:"
> "New every morning is the love:"
> "O Father, hear my morning prayer."

Just as the morning hymn should have something of the thrill of spiritual adventure, so *The Evening Hymn* should have something of spiritual peace: the restfulness of the dark, but certainly not its suggestion of the shadow of death. "Now the day is over" and "Sun of my soul" bring comfort. Bishop Wordsworth's "The day is gently sinking to a close" brings distress with its "The weary world is mouldering to decay" and "Onward to darkness and to death we tend": partial truths sentimentally draped, whose reiteration can bring help or health to no human soul. Our evening hymns need a drastic revision.

The Sunday Hymn used to vibrate between a seventh day of rest and a first day of resurrection. That is why, I suppose, Bishop Wordsworth's didactic "O day of rest and gladness" strives to explain the chronology. In a not especially rich department it is still perhaps, barring a depressing line or two, our best hymn.

The Hymn at the Opening of Service deserves more attention than it gets from pastors. It is psychologically important. The custom of opening with the L. M. doxology came down from New England, whence I fear the custom of sitting at prayer also came. In its own way it is equally inept. The doxology used to be the Te Deum of the unliturgical; reserved for occasion, sung with feeling. What has cheapened it and taken the heart out of it is the simple psychological truth that the late breakfast and scanning of the Sunday newspaper and the rush to be in time for church do not lay an adequate foundation for so lofty a burst of praise. When the doxology is so used I feel that the service never quite recovers from the *faux pas*. An opening hymn should take a lower level, that the service may ascend and not descend:

> "The earth is hushed in silence:"
> "This is the day of light:"
> "Lord, when we bend before Thy throne."
> "Spirit Divine, attend our prayer."

The Hymn at the Close of Service may be regarded liturgically as dismission or homiletically as the hymn after sermon. From the first point of view Ellerton's "Saviour, again to Thy dear Name we raise" is a most interesting blend of the corporate conception of worship with our human individuality. The congregation first sounds its corporate note of praise, and then on their "homeward way" severally ask God's blessing on their lives. It has been spoiled in the new Episcopal hymnal, but as given in the Presbyterian seems perfection.

Only a severe liturgiologist would refuse to yield the closing hymn to the preacher of the day who understands how to make use of it. It is an opportunity but a delicate task. He does not need a hymn on the same theme as his sermon, but kindred in tone and atmosphere, that shall seem like a melody the sermon evoked. As if, for instance, the sermon should argue for survival after death, and the congregation should respond not with a song of immortality but with a prayer that the Kindly Light may lead us in the dark:

Till "with the morn those angel faces smile
Which I have loved long since, and lost awhile."

Advent, which begins the Church Year, finds little recognition in non-liturgical communions, as a preparation for Christmas. *The Second Advent Hymn* seems likely to become the peculiar property of Premillenarians. No one can foretell whether they will go forward to establish the Advent season, or, like Horatius Bonar, aim to bathe the whole year in the light of expectation. Bonar's hymns alone furnish an ample Advent hymnody:

"Come, Lord, and tarry not:"
"Is the Bridegroom absent still:"
"Hark! 'tis the watchman's cry."

The Christmas Hymn came first into the home, then into the Sunday school, later into the church. In the index of subjects in the Presbyterian *Psalms and Hymns* of 1831 three Psalms are mentioned under "Incarnation," three hymns under "Nativity." In the 1843 book "Incarnation" heads a section of eleven more attractive hymns. Christmas hymnody has gradually assumed very full proportions. Influenced by a growing love of old carols it tends to reproduce the simplicities of their handling of the gospel of the Infancy rather than the splendor of the angels' song. It is represented by Phillips Brooks' "O little town of Bethlehem" rather than by Wesley's "Hark! the herald angels sing."

The Epiphany Hymn finds a use by merging it with Christmas carols; sometimes, I am afraid, from an unawareness of the difference in date and significance of the two occasions. Better so perhaps than that the coming of the Gentiles and all that it means should be overlooked. But the Epiphany surely is the great missionary occasion of the year.

The Palm Sunday Hymn is finding increasing use, and Holy week is gradually usurping the place of the old time Week of Prayer, set for the most inconvenient week of the year; very probably to avoid a seeming participation in Advent or Lent.

The Passion Hymn has fallen into considerable neglect,—an anomaly in communions that make much of the Atonement. It is regrettable that they have adopted Easter so much more enthusiastically and generally than Good Friday. Is a parish congregation that passes by the green hill without the city wall spiritually fitted to find the empty tomb? At a time when so many parishes made each Communion season something of a Good Friday celebration, the question was less pertinent than now. It has become rather critical in States that have, imprudently I think, made the day a legal holiday. In such case the Church's option is to encourage the people in the public sports that now mark an American holiday, or to call them to remember the passion of our Lord.

It may of course be argued that hymns that vividly renew the humiliations and sufferings of the Passion are more likely to call forth "tears, idle tears" from the sentimental than to stimulate the resolves that lie too deep for tears. Certainly they are not wholesome "for human nature's daily food." Perhaps such as merely harrow the feelings should not be used at all, and such as are helpful be reserved for a fit occasion when they express rather than depress the feelings. Presbyterian congregations at least should be given opportunity to sing Dr. Alexander's version of the great Good Friday hymn, "O sacred Head, now wounded" to the even greater "Passion Chorale," for there is none other that so reveals the sanctity of life.

The Easter Hymn came into our churches by way of the Sunday school. There are no liturgical Churches that make more of the Easter festival than do many of the congregations once trained to regard all Sundays as equally the day of our Lord's rising. The test of an Easter song is its ability to reproduce something of the wonder, first of all, and then the assurance that filled the disciples' hearts. Its appeal is to the feelings. And our one peerless Easter song is still the one whose literary claims are humble and whose music transcends the rules of ritual song:

> "Jesus Christ is risen to-day,
> Our triumphant holy day, Alleluia!"

Our Easter hymns demand a careful scrutiny lest they degenerate into noise and an effort to work up an artificial hysteria. For they have put into the hands of a witnessing Church a means of bearing that witness which for some reason is singularly effective. People from the Church's borders and beyond heed the call to her Easter services as to none other, and join heartily in the Easter hymns. I am disposed to think they have done more to keep the reality of Christ's resurrection alive to the class we designate as "the man in the street" than any other agency. Our apologetic discourses are not convincing; our "Christian Evidences" get no closer to everyday people than a treatise on trigonometry. But our Easter visitors are very susceptible to the heightened feeling of the congregation, the suggestion of confidence that rings in the poetry and music.

The Ascension Day Hymn suffers from the feeling that favors the use of such as are appropriate to the season, since Ascension Day, coming during the week, has found no place in the Church Year of nonliturgical communions. But it is quite available for the "Sunday after Ascension Day," and should be revived, "lest we forget."

The Whitsunday Hymn and *The Trinity Hymn*, on the other hand, have not suffered at all from the failure to observe Whitsunday and Trinity Sunday. Even the liturgical mind and temper would probably feel that Heber's "Holy! Holy! Holy! Lord God Almighty" and Miss Auber's "Our blest Redeemer, ere He breathed" may be encouraged to girdle the whole of the revolving church year.

In any communion or parish in which you or I are likely to serve we must accept the observance of church days as a fact accomplished. The observance has not come by inheritance or authority; and certainly not as a result of fruitful studies on the part of the clergy in liturgics, the most neglected amongst us of all theological disciplines. Nor is it a natural evolution or even a logical development. It is a partial reversion to the ideals and practices of other communions that have adhered to the liturgical conception of worship, and has been brought about by sentiment; responding in feeling to those influences, partly spiritual, partly esthetic, that started from the Oxford Revival.

Whether these influences will carry the liturgical movement to a complete adoption of the Church Year as the most seemly and convenient framework of worship and edification, or whether they will be counteracted by the informal spirit of evangelism or the free ways of modern life, who can predict of a movement so unguided and so immune from official interference?

For my own part I have been led to believe that the liturgical conception of hymnody is useful within its limits, and that the personal adoption by a pastor of a part of the Church Year, say from Advent to Whitsunday, is the most helpful guide in the important matter of his choice of hymns for his people. It centers church song around the various aspects of the person of Christ instead of the personality of the pastor, his whims and limitations or his indifference. It tends to widen the congregational repertoire, and to furnish an occasion and a setting, week by week, for the great hymns of the Church. But this end, and not the particular method of securing it, is the main thing.

For thirty years I have occupied a quasi-official relation to the hymnody of one communion, and am in a position to know how widespread the complaint, how deep the indignation at the manner in which so many of our pastors are using the hymnal. I may quote a communication (from an esteemed elder) that comes to me in the very act of this writing. "It is shocking," he says, "how our best ministers simply go around in a circle, picking out a few of the more familiar hymns that will fit the sermon they have just prepared." The administering of such a shock once or twice a week does seem an odd method of teaching and admonishing one another with Psalms and hymns and spiritual songs in such a way as will make melody in their hearts.

But the liturgical hymn exemplifies only one side of the churchly theory of hymnody we have been considering. The other and, I think, more helpful side, is in infusing our hymnody with a new sense of the solidarity of the Church: in setting beside the hymn of individual experience and duty the Church Hymn, which finds its inspiration in common membership of the Body of Christ, and answers His common call with common song.

This churchly conception has not made and cannot make the hymn to be simply the voice of the corporate Church, nor made it other than St. Paul made it, the spiritual song of a Christian heart. But it has made the common road of life and service resound with millions of voices joined in the marching song of a Catholic Church:

"We are not divided,
All one body we."

It has left a sectarian hymnody far behind. Toplady's polemic verses on Election would be no more welcome to a Presbyterian congregation than Wesley's on "The horrible decree" would be to a Methodist congregation. The modern hymnal is the nearest approach yet made to the unity of Christ's Church.

LECTURE FIVE

THE TEXT OF THE HYMNS

LECTURE FIVE

THE TEXT OF THE HYMNS

I. The Puritan Zeal for "Purity" of Text

The first book printed in this country was a psalm book.

The English Puritans who came to Massachusetts Bay in the seventeenth century brought with them the *Sternhold and Hopkins Psalter* they had used in their parish churches at home. Here, in the wilderness, far from the conventions of civilization, all alone with God, the familiar English psalm book raised, as most things did in that atmosphere, scruples of conscience. It dealt too loosely with the inspired Hebrew text. Whether the men who had made it lacked a sufficient acquaintance with that language, or felt the strain and shackles of versification, it was not literal. It lacked "purity."

And so a little group of emigrant scholars, cut off from most of life's comforts and most scholarly resources by the wide ocean, and threatened by savage neighbors, set themselves to the task of constructing a purer version of the Psalms in meter,—if meter it is to be called. Then they sent to the old home for a press and some fonts of type, and in 1640 printed their now famous *Bay Psalm Book*.

Their enterprise was quixotic, and the few copies

of their Psalm Book that survive are the most appealing memorial of what we now call the New England conscience. And it was all, we are tempted to say, by way of a pedantic concern for the text of their songs, a matter of the right word and the turn of a phrase.

That would be to overlook the fact that to the seventeenth century Puritan the text of their church-songs had come to mean everything. The metrical Psalm was to them not a hymn based on Scripture: it was a revised version of Scripture. Granting that principle of an inspired song discussed in a former lecture, were not the Church authorities bound first to provide and then safeguard a literal version of the Psalms that could be sung? The remote and romantic surroundings of the *Bay Psalm Book* make it an isolated cairn showing the extreme lengths to which a Puritan Church would go in this pursuit. But so far as the actual proceedings of the Bay divines are concerned, they were doing just what the General Assembly of the Church of Scotland did a very few years later in their protracted revision of "Rous' Version" of the Psalms before allowing the Scottish kirks to introduce it into public worship.

When the eighteenth century revival awakened New England, both the Psalms and hymns of Watts were in many hands and hearts already. The evangelical enthusiasm aroused by Whitefield's preaching cleared the hearers' minds of the earlier scruples and agitations concerning psalmody. The whole structure of Puritan psalmody gave way under evangelical pressure, and the singing of hymns started almost spontaneously.

It was now the Presbyterian churches that held on to Puritan traditions of psalmody, and even those who yielded to revival influences asked no more than permission to introduce Watts' version of the Psalms. The desolating Psalmody Controversy that ensued was, on the face of it, nothing more than a controversy concerning the text of Psalms. The practical issue was whether the parishes be restricted to the "Rous" version of the Scottish Assembly, just referred to, or might substitute Watts' free renderings of the substance of the Psalms, with their evangelical implications clearly expressed, and their text otherwise adapted to English feeling. The whole controversy relates itself to the original situation at Massachusetts Bay. The question raised was simply a new turn given to the Puritan scruple as to purity of the text.

In the Presbyterian Synod, as we all know, the accommodated Psalm as against the literal Psalm won through. The free hymn soon followed (as no doubt both parties had expected that it would) and was given full recognition in the *Directory for Worship* of 1788.

The new hymns quite naturally were an object of suspicion to those in any communion who questioned their use. Laying no claim to "purity" of text, they had all the more on that account to submit themselves to rigid scrutiny by responsible representatives of the Churches, and by amateur theologians, very numerous in those more thoughtful days. Even more they had to be watched and guarded against error by those who had made themselves responsible for their admission, and were hoping so much from their use.

The text of hymns was thus much more of a concern, when the time came to prepare new hymn books of their own make for the various communions in this country. And to the average Christian, who cherished the hymn book in his private devotions and learned many of the hymns by heart, their text meant a great deal more than that of such poetry as he read, and which he could take or leave. It meant more than the text of Shakespeare means to a scholar, just because it came closer to his life.

II. The Textual Criticism of Our Hymns

In 1860, when hymn books were aplenty, Dr. Park and Dr. Phelps of Andover Seminary published their *Hymns and Choirs*,[1] a book still instructive, and retaining the distinction of being the first American attempt at a systematic hymnology. In view of what has just been said it is not surprising that a good deal more than a third of the book deals with "The Text of Hymns." The treatise is really an *apologia* for *The Sabbath Hymn Book* its authors had published two years earlier after more years of careful preparation, and with a knowledge of the subject that in its time and place was probably unique. They had sought out many new hymns and had subjected the familiar ones to close criticism, constructing in many cases a text of their own, involving omissions, amendments and even additions.

Their hymn book encountered a storm of criticism, in which the publishers of Elias Nason's *Congregational Hymn Book*,[2] recently put on the market, took the part of Æolus. And of course the changes of familiar texts afforded the most vulnerable point of attack: and it became incumbent upon the authors of *Hymns and Choirs* to justify them.

It is possible therefore that the ample space allotted to "The Text of Hymns" in their treatise does not correspond precisely with their sense of proportion in constructing a hymnological system. Very likely it measures the extent of their chagrin at the reception their amended texts had met. Be that as it may the chapter remains the fullest presentation of the subject yet given. It is from the hand of Professor Park and is worked out with the precision and particularity to be expected from that hand. If one could reduce his many categories to more manageable bounds, the lines of his thesis would be something like these:

(a) *That the criticism of hymns is as necessary as it is perilous.* [The peril he had been forcibly made to realize. The necessity he would no doubt impress upon many whose memory enshrined this or that text of familiar hymns learned in childhood, and who resented any changes of text without regard to their meritoriousness].

(b) *That an immense number of textual alterations are present in current hymn books:* [in all practically, though Dr. Park kept the "Old School Presbyterian Collection" well to the fore by way of illustration].

(c) *That changes of text are really desirable for various reasons:* [that range all the way from the sphere of sound doctrine to that of elementary grammar: and which he proceeds to catalogue and to illustrate with a wealth of detail].

(d) *That all the omissions and amendments of text in "The Sabbath Hymn Book" are justified.* This last, the heart of the discussion to Dr. Park and his colleague, has ceased to beat, now that their book lies buried beneath the strata of time. You cannot expect a wide public to take an interest in fossil remains, and yet both fossil and book are links in the chain of life, and each has a story to tell. If discriminating sermons were still wanted, a preacher could find many a theme in the alteration of hymn texts which the Andover Faculty thought necessary or desirable in 1858.

III. The Confusing State of the Text

The only one of Dr. Park's propositions that was incontestable was that revealing the multitude of divergences in the text of the Psalms and hymns then in current use. It was not merely that so many differed from what their authors had written: there was a lack of uniformity in the text of even the cherished hymns as given in various books and sung in different congregations. Of most of them there was in fact no standard text and the clamorous or pathetic appeal against any alteration had little to rest upon other than prejudice or individual association.

"There is," he says, "a multitude of readers who rely implicitly on the text of the Presbyterian (Old School) Collection, and regard every instance of departure from this text as a violation of the rights of authorship; yet in seven hundred and forty of the more common lyrics in that Collection, there are thirteen hundred and twenty-seven variations, exclusive of the frequent omissions. In the preface or advertisement of that manual it is stated: 'The psalms have been left without alteration; the Committee believing that it would be extremely difficult to furnish a more acceptable version than that of Watts. . . .' But in the three hundred and forty-five versions of psalms contained in the Collection, there are six hundred and ninety-seven alterations.

Indeed there are not one hundred and ten of these psalms unaltered." [3]

In the New School Presbyterian hymn book, Professor Park found thirteen hundred and thirty-six variations of the original text in seven hundred and seventy-four of its most noted hymns. Of books used in Congregationalist churches he found eleven hundred and twenty-six changes in eight hundred and ten familiar hymns of the Connecticut Association's book, and nine hundred changes in five hundred and fifty hymns he examined in Henry Ward Beecher's *Plymouth Collection.*

These figures are hard to grasp and to retain, but they leave an impression of the actual state of the hymns then in use. That impression may perhaps be deepened by selecting the single case of a hymn whose words lie familiarly in the memory of most of us: Toplady's "Rock of Ages, cleft for me." So it began in Presbyterian and Congregationalist churches; but many Baptist congregations, who used Rippon's *Selection,*[4] were singing "Rock of Ages, shelter me"; and Episcopalian, Methodist and Lutheran congregations were using a recast of the four verses into three.

Old School Presbyterians were singing "From Thy wounded side which flowed."
New School Presbyterians were singing "From Thy riven side which flowed."
Some Congregationalists were singing "From Thy side a healing flood."

Old School—"Cleanse me from its guilt and power."
New School—"Save me, Lord, and make me pure."
Some Congregationalists—"Save from wrath, and make me pure."

Old School—"Could my zeal no respite know."
New School—"Should my zeal no languor know."

Old School—"Nothing in my hand I bring."
New School—"In my hand no price I bring."

Old School—"See Thee on Thy judgment-throne."
New School—"And behold Thee on Thy throne."

These are but some of the variances in the text of a single hymn. They are brought forward here, if you will remember, simply to illustrate the fact that in the texts of the body of hymns that grew up here and was sung in the eighteen sixties, let us say, and which was the inheritance of my generation, there were countless divergences from the author's text and variant readings even of the emendations. There was a striking lack of uniformity. There was no common text, even among Old and New School Presbyterians, or among Baptists or Congregationalists.

This state of things made itself felt as an annoyance to anybody who really cared for the hymns and a great embarrassment when different groups of Christian people tried to sing together. But the actual situation was little apprehended then by those who blamed it on the compilers of their hymn books, and is not very generally understood even now. It is perhaps worthwhile therefore to ask how it happened that the text of our hymnody fell into such a state.

IV. The Causes of This Confusion

Dr. Watts was not actually the first writer who aimed to ameliorate the Psalms by injecting evangelical interpretations into their text. But his *The Psalms of David imitated* (1719) must be held responsible for the project of making the whole structure of the Psalter and the substance of its text a framework on which to weave an evangelical psalmody of mingled praise and British patriotism; and all in David's name, now, as Watts put it, converted from a Jew into a Christian. In the face of such proposal the recent efforts of a Weymouth or a Moffatt to give us a Bible in modern English impress us by their restraint.

Who would imagine that in the following lines Dr. Watts is giving us the opening of the 75th Psalm:

> "*Britain* was doom'd to be a Slave,
> Her Frame dissolv'd; her Fears were great;
> When God a new Supporter gave
> To bear the Pillars of the State."

It is much easier to understand the violent protests of Romaine and others aroused by such a handling of the sacred text than it is to explain how these accommodations and modernizations were gravely accepted by the churches in lieu of more literal versions, yet still "Psalms." But such was the case.

Watts' *Psalms imitated* were reprinted in the American colonies up to the time of the Revolution without change of text. But with the dawn of the spirit of independence his frequent allusions to Britain and King George wore out their welcome. I have copies of early American imprints in which they are erased and more patriotic phrases inserted by the pen of some one, probably a precentor. After the Revolution the Connecticut Association employed Joel Barlow to revise Watts' text and to accommodate it to American worship. After several editions of this, Barlow fell into such personal disrepute that the Association engaged President Dwight to make a fresh rescension. The Presbyterian Synod had already adopted Barlow's revision, and now the General Assembly approved Dr. Dwight's. Dr. Worcester soon followed with an independent rescension of his own. So that there were in circulation at once Barlow's revision of Watts' Psalms, partly superseded in Connecticut, but adhered to by Presbyterians, almost universally in Pennsylvania and New Jersey; Dr. Dwight's revision, favored by Connecticut Congregationalists who distrusted Barlow and by many Presbyterians, especially in New York; and Dr. Worcester's revision, favored in New England, especially Massachusetts. The textual confusion was further increased by several publishers who got out editions of their own, which adopted emendations from these three revisions, with some further changes, made possibly with a view of avoiding the infringement of copyrights.[5]

Turning now to Watts' *Hymns*—he had expressed in his preface, and perhaps felt, a willingness that his words should not be regarded as sacred. The leader of worship should be at liberty to substitute a better for an "unpleasing" word: it was the day when hymns were given out line by line by the precentor. "We are not," he said, "confined to the words of any one man in our public solemnities."

But he could not have anticipated the drastic changes his texts underwent at the hands of the English Presbyterians in their progress to declared Unitarianism. These Arian rescensions were still printed under Watts' name, and without intimation that they had been changed. The protest this aroused among orthodox contemporaries was met by the claim that they, the Unitarians, were doing to Watts just what Watts had done to "David," and what Watts himself would have done had he rewritten the hymns according to his changed views in later years. An Arian text of Watts was thus set up and justified, in time to be a precedent for our Massachusetts Unitarians.

When there was a prospect of introducing human compositions into Scottish Presbyterian worship, the successive committees on Hymns and Paraphrases wrestled with the text of them just as their fathers had with "Rous' Version," and they produced a Scottish rescension of some of Watts' hymns that has become more familiar than the original text.

But in a wide circle of Independent and other churches Watts' *Hymns* were regarded with a reverence that kept their text sacrosanct. They were accepted not individually but *en masse*, as in themselves a complete hymnal; their number, their arrangement "in three books" and their text, all unchanged. It is striking, certainly, that in Boston as late as 1819, a hundred and twelve years after their publication, Dr. Worcester's attempt in his *Christian Psalmody* to present some abridgment and alteration of the *Hymns* encountered a resentment so great that his publishers had to recall the book and insist on restoring "Watts entire," as it was then called, without abridgment or alteration of a word.

And yet many of the hymns cried aloud either for exclusion or for some amendment; there was so much careless composition, so many breaches of good taste. How could a critical editor be expected, for instance, to approve an expression of the Christmas situation such as that of the 13th hymn of the first book:

"This infant is the mighty God,
Come to be suckled and adored."

Even this Dr. Worcester was compelled to restore

in his later book, known as *Worcester's Watts*. The committees who compiled the Presbyterian *Psalms and Hymns* of 1831 and 1843 handled the hymns of Watts more selectively and more critically, amending where they could not admire.

John Wesley, a warm admirer of Watts, had from the first felt no more hesitation in altering his text than in blue-penciling his brother's hymns or adapting the poems of George Herbert. Not even that deft hand could make Herbert congregational. But his method vindicated itself permanently in dealing with Watts' ineffective 100th Psalm, beginning:

"Sing to the Lord with joyful voice;
Let every land his Name adore,
The British isles shall send the noise
Across the ocean to the shore:"

which he transformed into the fine hymn:

"Before Jehovah's awful throne,
Ye nations, bow with sacred joy."

John Wesley desired that the text of his brother's and his own hymns, furnished in his large *Collection of Hymns for . . . Methodists* (1780) should be final. As for hymn tinkerers, he said in the preface, "I desire they would not attempt to mend them; for they really are not able. None of them is able to mend either the sense or the verse." The reference here very likely was to Whitefield and Toplady, both of whom had altered the hymns they appropriated. After Wesley's death his wishes were disregarded even by the publishers of his own book. Charles Wesley's hymns suffered long at editorial hands that were all thumbs. His "Jesu, Lover of my soul," being the most lyrical, suffered most, and only in our day has been restored to its original beauty.

The poet Montgomery in his anthologies and hymn books covered the whole range of materials available at the opening of the nineteenth century with his purpose to elevate the literary standard of praise. With a self-confidence as great as Wesley's, he was even freer of hand than Wesley. In editing Cotterill's book of 1819[6] he put into circulation many modified texts. It was he who changed Cowper's "There is a fountain filled with blood" to "From Calvary's cross a fountain flows," and who made the 3-verse rescension of "Rock of Ages" that so long prevailed in English and American Episcopal Churches. He said that the time and thought he gave to amending the Moravian hymn book would have sufficed for the composition of a like quantity of original verse. And he predicted quite truly that when he was gone his own hymns would be "altered to suit the taste of appropriators."

With Montgomery we are come down to the nineteenth century and to a period when hymn books began to multiply on all sides in the effort of enlarging or freshening the service of song in various communions. And with this multiplication of books the confusion of text became worse confounded. Partly because every compiler felt the duty of conforming the materials at hand to the doctrinal beliefs of his constituency. Partly also because he felt free to alter any expression not commending itself to his judgment or his whims.

But the great cause of confusion lay deeper.

V. The First Attempts to Verify the Texts

All these compilers of hymn books were working in the dark, with very little knowledge of their materials. Apart from reprints of Watts and *Olney Hymns* in circulation, the sources were vague, or, if known, quite inaccessible. A new book was made up from such earlier and current selections as its compiler had on hand. The guess-work or blunder of one compiler as to the authorship or text of the hymns became the assurance of the next. The emendations of one compiler, made freely and unacknowledged, became the original text to the one copying it into the later book. And for such an enterprise a pair of shears and a blue pencil seemed equipment enough. In the complacency behind such a statement as that of the compilers of the Presbyterian *Psalms and Hymns* of 1843 that they had determined to adhere to the text of Watts' revision of the Psalms, their ignorance, in view of the not remote contests and excitements within their own communion, can only be described as willful. Certainly it was abysmal. The thought that the matter of preparing the Church's songs called for anything in the nature of scholarship was slow to dawn. The Andover Faculty caught the light, and pursued it. Some hymn books from Dr. Park's library with his annotations, now in my possession, show his concern and suggest how limited were his resources.

Strange as it may seem to-day Roundell Palmer's *Book of Praise*, published at London and New York, in 1862, was the first attempt to recover and restore the original text of our hymns. Even this could not have been made without the help of Daniel Sedgwick, a second-hand bookseller of London. The flotsam of literature drifted his way, and he thought it worth while (he was the first who did) to collect and collate the old Psalm and hymn books; until, as Palmer said, "he knew more about them and their authors than any one else" then living.[7]

The Book of Praise proved an incentive to a wider inquiry into sources and texts. Sedgwick's little shop became its center, and he the oracle to whom for many years the more ambitious hymnal editor was accustomed to resort.

During the next thirty years the study advanced so far that it became possible for Dr. John Julian, Vicar of Wincobank, to assemble quite a group of scholars in preparing his *Dictionary of Hymnology*, published in 1891. This was at once a survey of and a guide to what had been a very roughly charted territory.

With the *Dictionary* at hand the least industrious compiler could now give the authorship and date of a great number of his hymns. But that is as far as such a book could serve. Except in a few cases of unusual interest it could not within its limits reproduce the texts of the hymns. And the sources remain difficult of access. Dr. Julian himself was obliged to go to press without having seen a copy of the original edition of either Watts' *Hymns* or his *Horæ Lyricæ*, and was therefore unaware of the many variances of text in different issues of these books. Not even a thesaurus has been made of English hymns, such as Koch and Wackernagel have made of the German, and Dreves and Blume of the Latin. Nor is there likely to be. The mass of the materials is so overwhelming, and much of it so unrewarding from any standpoint.

Editorial work of the right sort had been done before Julian's day by such men as Charles Rogers, Godfrey Thring and Canon Ellerton, and in this country notably by Frederic M. Bird, the first extensive collector here of the sources.

But on the whole it is not unfair to say that the textual confusion and uncertainty already described at some length was not greatly relieved when the General Assembly of the Presbyterian Church in the U. S. A. gave to its Board of Publication the instructions which eventuated somewhat tardily in *The Hymnal* of 1895.

VI. The Textual Canons of 1895

We are now in a position to discuss intelligently what we may call the textual canons of our hymnody. Instead of dealing with them in the abstract I propose now to bring to a focus this whole matter of the text—its purity, its modifications, its acceptability—by way of restating the actual principles by which the text of *The Hymnal* of 1895 was constructed.

Perhaps I ought to begin with an attempt to justify such proposal.

In view of the conditions shown, those to whom the project of the new hymnal was committed could hardly fail to feel the need of a fresh study of the text of the whole body of our hymnody in use, and the opportunity for an attempt to put it on a firmer basis.

Their field was clear. They were neither helped nor hampered by traditional texts common to all who were likely to make use of the new church hymnal; many of whom indeed had given up the use of authorized books in favor of one or another of Dr. Charles S. Robinson's, with whom textual criticism was not a strong point. They were also confronted by what may be called "the awful example" of the new Protestant Episcopal hymnal of 1891, whose textual vagaries are still unexplained. It is enough to say here that in that book "Nearer, my God, to Thee" was relieved of all allusion to Jacob's dream: that "My Country, 'tis of thee" was cut in half, and the half joined on to "God bless our native land" to make a whole: and that Cowper's "Hark! my soul, it is the Lord," was so dealt with that the cultured Dr. Huntington, who had loved it, was heard to declare he could never give it out again in Grace Church.

Obviously the work on the hymns considered for the new book should begin, where scholarship of any sort begins, with a first-hand knowledge of the sources. And so a systematic search began for all the books or periodicals in which the hymns first appeared and the hymn books whose rescension of them completed their textual history.

When these had been gathered up in England and this country to the fullest extent possible to enterprise and patience, the way was opened to the construction of an acceptable text, whether by restoration or amendment. And that brings us to the textual principles of 1895.

1. *The General Principle of Conformity*

The general principle was that the hymns should be printed as their authors wrote them, so far as practicable. Why otherwise all this trouble and expense in procuring the originals?

In our modern study of poetry, bibliographical and textual research has subordinated esthetic study. In the critical editions of the poets replacing the trade editions one by one, the recovery of what the poet actually wrote is the common *motif* and the one achievement. The comments of Dr. Johnson and his kind are superseded by bibliographical adjustments and variorum readings, in an attempt to determine the true text. And this zeal for what the author wrote shines alike on the good and evil that he did. In Amy Lowell's vast book on John Keats a caustic estimate of the ineptitude of some passage or line will be followed by a burst of indignation at some known or unknown hand that has ventured on some trifling change in it.

Clearly this zeal for what the author wrote is the paramount feeling. And it is just as reasonable, and just as right, in hymnody as in poetry. The ethics of quotation support it, and very often the emendations made in our hymns justify it. Some of these were conscientiously made by way of diluting poetic expressions to suit the palate of Dr. Watts' "meanest Christian." Some, as has been said here, represent no more than an editor's whimsies. "It is astonishing," as Montgomery said, "how really religious persons will sometimes feel scruples about a turn or a term."[8] Other of these textual changes are no more than the inadvertences of frequent reprintings and careless proof-reading.

There is an instance of this in the version of the

100th Psalm which is the foundation stone of our hymnody:

"All people that on earth do dwell."

It was first printed in 1560-1, and taken into the English Psalter in 1564. One line had read, "We are his folk, he doth us feed" [his folk, his *people;* spelt folck]. Within a year the transposing of a single letter by a type-setter made the word "flock"; and so the text stood for 317 years until the Rev. Godfrey Thring discovered the error.

So Charles Wesley's hymn, which he made to commence,

"Love Divine, all loves excelling,"

soon began to pass current as "all love excelling," not because anybody thought God's love excelled love itself, but only because an "s" dropped out. It happened that the restoration of this one letter drew forth numerous letters of protest in 1895, but it was right nevertheless.

And this particular instance brings us back to the rightness of the general principle that what an author wrote is to be preferred as far as practicable. Especially so if the author was a poet. How intolerable have been the editorial changes in "Jesu, Lover of my soul" and "Lead, Kindly Light!"

Nevertheless there is that "as far as practicable," which separates and always must separate the anthology from the hymn book. In a collection of poems for poetry's sake the rule of fidelity of text is absolute. In a collection of hymns for congregational use the fidelity must be tempered by considerations of practical utility. There is no real use in playing the part of "superior" in this matter or in increasing the hue and cry after the fleeing "hymn-tinkerer." When all has been said and the tinkerer impounded, the regrettable necessity of making certain adjustments of materials abides.

2. *The Limits of the Principle of Conformity*

The judicial pronouncements making the rule of conformity absolute come from those who administer the theory rather than the practice of hymnody. They would preserve the rights of an author at all hazards. These rights are certainly sacred. The editor of 1895 tried to verify them by getting the author's actual text into his own hands, and to preserve them by the simple expedient of noting beneath each hymn every deviation from the original; that an author's name should be attached to nothing he did not write.

The deviations then allowed may conveniently be studied under two heads: (1) A privilege of abridgment; (2) A necessity of amendments.

(a) ABRIDGMENT. The privilege of making omissions from the text is allowable even in an anthology, and in a hymnal is indispensable.

When Metrical Psalmody was made a church ordinance in France and the Netherlands, the principle of conformity to Scripture demanded that the Psalter be sung through in its integrity. It was enough to insert the word "Pause" into longer Psalms to indicate where practicable divisions could be made.

No one who knows our modern sources could suggest a similar principle of inclusiveness. "Sun of my soul" consists of selected verses from one of the opening poems of Keble's *Christian Year* which is not a hymn. "Jerusalem the golden" covers sixteen lines of a satire that runs to nearly three thousand. Symond's "These things shall be! a loftier race" begins with the fourth verse of a poem that has seventeen. The best of Whittier's hymns are likewise extracted from long poems.

Some of our hymns contain in themselves matter that is extraneous or unwelcome, best disposed of by omission. That is true even of so great a hymn as "When I survey the wondrous cross": better in four verses than in five.

More commonly it is simply the undue length of a hymn that demands curtailment. The longest of all, "Dies irae" escapes, because it remains in our hymnals as mainly a great historical monument, which must not be mutilated. The next in length, perhaps, is Byrom's "Christians, awake! salute the happy morn"; desirable for its out-of-doors flavor and its fine music,—but what an interminable narrative! Every editor feels called to attack the problem of curtailment: none feels that he has solved it.

The proper length of a hymn would seem to be a matter for care and good judgment. In practice it is too often determined by the amount of space available in making up the page of the hymnal. The rule adhered to in 1895 was to present each hymn with the brevity of a good lyric and with the integrity of a good hymn; that is to say, with sufficient fullness to preserve its message and to complete its development.

The case is simple enough surely. A hymn has to make a quick impression, to carry it forward, and to heighten it to a spiritual uplift. A good hymn therefore has these three structural characteristics:

(1) An opening that catches the attention and plays the same part that a theme does in a piece of music;

(2) A continuous development and unbroken advance in which one verse rises on the stepping-stones of its predecessors;

(3) A climax in which the theme is triumphant, and the advance has won its goal.

Now this structure is not academic but experiential. It is based on the psychology of attention which loses as soon as it begins to ramble. Any mechanical or ill-judged shortening snaps this thread of continuity, and so weakens the appeal upon the attention of the verses that remain.

So far as the practice of singing is concerned perhaps the chief thing for an editor or pastor to remember relative to a hymn's length is that the quickened pace of modern singing and the cutting out of once prevalent interludes make practicable a much fuller representation of the text than was desirable a generation or so ago.

(b) Amendment. A necessity of amendment remains even after selection has secured the hymns consonant with the beliefs and ideals of those who are to use the hymnal. It is very limited. The hymns that have touched the common heart are naturally those that keep to the common ground. The familiar hymn that caused most concern in 1895 was Draper's "Ye Christian heralds, go proclaim," with its assurance of the immunity of missionaries from attack by the forces of nature. A slight modification turned the verses into a prayer for their protection. Monsell's "On our way rejoicing" had a line, "Clouds are not from Thee," that seemed an inadequate interpretation of a cloudy day, recalling the futile debate roused by Cuthbert Hall's *Does God send Trouble?*, and was made to read, "There is light in Thee." And the line, "Let us find the second rest," in Charles Wesley's "Love Divine, all loves excelling" became, more acceptably, "Let us find the promised rest." It would seem a pity if hymns so good should be debarred from general use for the sake of retaining an unguarded phrase.

It is possible to go so far as that with the feeling that the revered authors are looking down upon us with an understanding smile. But just how far may we go, say in the name of decency, in altering an author's personal beliefs by way of adapting his work to our own uses?

The most casuistic answer ever given to that question was that of James Martineau, who stands high among thinkers and quite supreme as a practitioner of the gentle art of hymn-tinkering. He expressed his conviction that the dogmatic content of Christian poetry was an accident and not an essential of its excellence. He said that in the book he was preparing he aimed in his alterations of text "to give theologically a translation but in respect to piety and poetry the precise originals of the several authors."[9] The English Unitarians had made themselves somewhat conspicuous in the art of "translation" thus indicated. And if this be the justification of their practice it is calculated to expand rather than to mollify the feeling of irritation we must all have experienced at finding some favorite hymn thus "translated" in some current Unitarian book.

But if we find Martineau's justification, to speak frankly, a bit shocking, then in what terms are we to justify our own appropriation of Father Faber's "Faith of our fathers! living still," and our "translation" of its doctrine into terms of Protestant polemics?

Faber's verses are a yearning plea for the restoration of the Roman Catholic faith of the fathers:

"Faith of our Fathers! Mary's prayers
Shall win our country back to thee;
And through the truth that comes from God
England shall then indeed be free."

The question of adopting the Protestant "translation" was up already in 1895, but rejected, out of self-respect shall I say, or in the interests of sincerity? In the revision of 1911 the hymn was admitted not from any change of judgment but in obedience to a demand so general as to leave no choice in the matter except between that of printing it in *The Hymnal revised* or on a separate leaflet that could be bound in with it. And so in this instance the authorized hymnal of an aggressively Protestant communion occupies by compulsion of its pastors the position of Dr. Martineau. The almost simultaneous adoption of the Roman Catholic lyric by Presbyterians and Unitarians offers an interesting study in comparative religion.

Faber's verses are not particularly good. They are redeemed poetically by the passion of his longing for the supremacy of the cult of the Virgin Mary. Protestantism may still hope for a eulogy on the faith of *its* fathers that may be sung without appealing to one's sense of humor.

Apart from matters of doctrine there are lines here and there, unhappy or unmetrical, that have lingered too long. In Watts for instance—the repeated "What worthless worms are we" in his "Great God, how infinite art Thou!"; "For such a worm as I" in "Alas! and did my Saviour bleed"; "He shall be damned that won't believe" in his "Go, preach my gospel, saith the Lord." In such cases the choice practically is between amendment and discard.

In respect of metrical irregularity, the trouble is not with the syllabification or what are called peculiar meters. If the rhythm is clearly marked, these need cause no more trouble in the church than the irregularities of Mother Goose cause in the nursery. Therefore in 1895 "O come, all ye faithful" and "One sweetly solemn thought" were released from the strait-jackets into which they had been compressed, and "Thou didst leave Thy throne and Thy kingly crown," with Tennyson's "Sunset and evening star" were admitted; the latter for the first time in an American book. The altered form of the first line of Neale's "The day of resurrection" was left standing because grown familiar, but the original " 'Tis the day of resurrection" would not embarrass the humblest singer.

The difficulty begins when some accent is wrong, or from a change of rhythm due to careless composition. Who has not suffered from the false accent on "Mortals" in Charles Wesley's "Rejoice, the Lord is king"? But it was left standing till 1911, through an exaggerated regard for the original.

More serious are the changes of rhythm in Monsell's "Light of the world, we hail Thee"; and I am now fully convinced that no tune can grapple with them. But they were suffered there as in all books since, so far as I know.

It was indeed, I now think, a fault of the text of 1895 that it made too little use of the privilege of amendment. The vast preponderance of the alterations were restorations of what the author originally wrote or adoptions of changes already made to a hymn's advantage. It was the fault of an over-scrupulosity in respecting the original texts, natural enough to a reaction from the uninformed and careless methods of its predecessors. With more than thirty years of added experience, I should not now hesitate to go much further: to relieve "All hail the power of Jesus' Name" of those vexing phrases; to recast a hymn so unwholesome as "O Paradise! O Paradise!"; and to deliver our hymnody in general from that preoccupation with death that broods over it like a shadow still in spite of all the winnowings it has had.[10]

In acknowledging its limitations it is only fair to add that *The Hymnal* of 1895 and 1911 has exerted a marked influence both in the choice of hymns and in their presentation. It has introduced many into common use. No less than five communions have asked formal permission to make use of its researches and its texts. And it has served elsewhere as an unacknowledged source-book for many hymnals; thus contributing somewhat toward the formation of a common text.

In this lecture I have tried to show that Hymnology as well as Letters must be allowed its own little department of textual criticism; that our church songs have a textual history, and must submit to canons framed for special ends. We have studied the canons governing a certain book, as illustrative and perhaps suggestive. But they are not final. Other books—other canons and other texts; and a new generation will do its own mending when once more time shall have frayed the text.

I should like to leave an impression that the state of the text is a matter of some importance. Of an importance only relative from a purely literary standpoint; not to be compared with that centering in a Horace or a Chaucer; but of some human interest, to say the least, and of great concern to the Church, when we think of the high offices our hymns are called upon to fill.

For, if the teaching power of hymns is very great, their words are the vehicle of the teaching. If congregational feeling is better expressed through hymnody than aught else, then what we have called the text is nothing less than that expression.

It is a far cry to days when synods and even national parliaments wrestled over the textual integrity or textual revision of church song. But there must be a middle ground between overzeal and the indifference into which the matter has been allowed to lapse in our modern parishes.

In a long oversight of the correspondence between the publishing house of the Presbyterian Church and the authorities of parishes considering the introduction of a new hymn book, I have been impressed by the absence from these parochial letters of any allusions to this matter of the text of the several books they may have had under comparison. Of course those who adopt the authorized hymnal of their communion may find no occasion to set forth their reasons. Those choosing some other book do as a rule mention the features that commend it. Among them I cannot recall a single instance in which the state of the text in which the hymns were offered for use appeared to have received any consideration or to have influenced the decision. The only exception, if it be such, was the case I am about to refer to, of a pastor preferring a book in which the hymns generally had been abridged.

3. *The Latest Menace to the Integrity of Our Hymns*

Just now the spiritual and literary integrity of our hymns is menaced by considerations that are purely mechanical.

The American hymnals of the eighteen fifties set the fashion of printing the tune across the top of the page and filling the space beneath with hymns corresponding in meter, arranged in double columns and closely packed. This necessitated some padding when the materials fell short, but also some trimming of the hymns when the materials were over long; and the length of a hymn became a typographical consideration.

In the Episcopal Church the hymns are adopted by General Convention without reference to their tunes, and arranged without grouping the meters, so that when a musical edition followed a changed typography was required; a free and open page in which each hymn could be dealt with separately and given whatever space it required. This arrangement was adopted for *The Hymnal* of 1895, and was largely responsible for the welcome it received. Until lately all the better type of hymnals for church use adopted this arrangement.

But the newer books are following the pattern set forth in the ephemeral song books of printing all the words of the hymns between the staves of the tunes. This expedient arose from the singer's difficulty in mating the rapid and rollicking tunes to the words provided, the words in many cases being evidently little more than pegs to hang the musical notes on.

There are, of course, hymns so irregular in meter that a real difficulty arises in setting the syllables to the proper notes, and in this case there does seem to exist a reason for printing the words parallel to the music; but to make this setting-up the standard of the hymns in general is open to three objections that ought to be final to any one who cares for the things of the spirit.

(a) The words strung out in long lines stretching across the page cease to be poetry; for poetry is a form as well as a spirit. Even Whitman and his followers insist on retaining the line arrangement, understanding quite well that even free verse must have the look of poetry. No one would, if he could escape, read the long strings of words crowded between the staves of these new books. And hymns that are not made personally familiar by devotional reading have not much spiritual influence.

(b) The unreadable words printed within the staves thus serve only as a libretto to the music. They are a direct contribution to that thoughtless singing of glib tunes we sometimes mistake for spiritual song. Where the music is catching or so rapid as to require attention, I have ascertained by actual questioning that it is only too common to sing the tune through to the syllables beneath in practical unconsciousness of any particular meaning in the words.

(c) The printing of the words between the staves involves the shortening of the hymns for purely mechanical reasons. Four verses begin to be a little inconvenient; five verses cause eyestrain; six verses are almost impracticable.

Now a good hymn is not a collection of stanzas. It has an architecture symmetrical from base to tower. It has a lyrical movement, progressing and culminating in a climax. The proposal to reduce our hymns to a four-verse common denominator was first made by the English Arians when the singing was slow and their spiritual affections cold. It awakened protest and approval and one or more editors ventured to apply the standard to Church of England hymn books. Hymnologists hitherto have regarded these ineffectual books with amusement, and cited them as "awful examples."

But now, one of the most recent church hymnals, apparently a successful one, is being advertised as desirable on the ground of setting the hymns between the staves of the music. And on examination I find that of the five hundred hymns of this book only forty-seven have more than four verses.

I do not know in just what words that will not fall short of urbanity to characterize this disregard of the spiritual integrity and the poetical development of our hymns for no reason whatever except for mechanical considerations. It is, of course, a phenomenon that has passed over from the side of modern religious song that is admittedly illiterate and demonstrably decadent.

Let us hope it will not pass far into the fair field of church song. It may be a fad, but it has already become a menace. In the particular communion with which I am connected it has begun to affect the higher interests of church song.

A number of parochial committees have recently rejected the church hymnal because not printed in the new manner. Even a larger number of pastors are asking for an edition of *The Hymnal* so printed; a thing impossible because no typographical ingenuity can force the full form of many hymns within the brace and have it still usable. And on the day before writing these words the climax arrives in a request from a pastor to issue an edition of *The Hymnal*, with all the hymns reduced to four verses, as consuming less time in worship.

I do not like to end on so low a note, which sounds as though I were accusing my brethren of a lack of culture. So, I shall make mine own the more gracious words with which a distinguished bishop lately ended the account of his observation of some other modern features of Presbyterian worship: "It takes culture," he said, "a long time to arrive at expression."

LECTURE SIX

HYMN SINGING

LECTURE SIX

HYMN SINGING[1]

I. The Hymn and the Hymn Tune

So far we have been dealing in the main with hymnody as a body of religious verse furnishing the subject-matter for congregational song, without special reference to the tunes which are as essential as the hymns themselves in the actual practice of hymnody. In thus postponing until now any consideration of the hymn tune we have simply followed the logic of the situation. Any words chosen to be sung have a natural priority over the music they are to be set to and the act of singing them.

But in the case of our hymns the logical priority of their words over their tunes is immensely emphasized. The body of its hymnody is primarily the sacred poetry of the Christian religion; the record of the highest appropriations of truth and the flowers of Christian experience, gathered out of all ages of the Church and conveyed through the appealing medium of verse. The verse, just because it is lyrical, is so much the easier to read and remember. To a considerable body of the brotherhood hymnody is the only religious poetry that counts, if not indeed the only poetry, apart from the newspaper waifs and strays, with which they come into personal contact.

It is as devotional verse rather than as song that our hymns have entered into the spiritual experience of a myriad hymn lovers, to whom the church hymnal has meant most as the companion of silent hours, the source of remembered inspirations. It would be as futile to contend that Christian hymns have no office and no message until sung in the congregation as to say that the poetical and spiritual uplift of *The Book of Psalms* was confined to the comparatively few Jews who participated in the Temple worship.

It is more to the point to say that it is only the precedent appropriation of the hymn's message by each individual heart that makes its congregational singing worthwhile. It is the truths and experiences expressed in them that makes the music to which they are sung to be religious music.

Except in intent and through association there can hardly be such a thing as Christian music. Indeed if we are to divide life into compartments and set apart only one as dedicated to religion, it is questionable if there is such a thing as distinctively religious music. There is of course carnal and spiritual music. But in music that is pure in feeling and uplifting who can draw the line between secular and religious? Until it be clothed in words who can say whether the strains that incite us to activity incite us to the activities of brotherhood or the struggle for supremacy; whether the music that brings visions of peace points to Nirvana or to Heaven? Schumann's *Nachtstücke No.* 4 is secular, I suppose; but as embodied in our tune, "Canonbury," it is a fit vehicle of religious expression. Sullivan's "St. Gertrude" would serve as a march of the marines in *Pinafore:* if it is religious, it is the somewhat spectacular Christianity of Baring-Gould's "Onward, Christian soldiers" that transmutes it.

It is then the thought and feeling of the hymn that imparts anything like a specifically religious tone to the music to which it is set. It would seem to follow that any theory of hymnody that subordinates the hymn to the hymn tune is definitely unchristian: and that any tendency in our hymn books or choir lofts to treat the words of our hymns as a mere libretto of the music, however beautiful it be, should be dealt with very frankly.

We have already before us sufficient materials for a rationale of the hymn tune. We have first of all the hymn whose message, being spiritual, is necessarily, like the gospel itself, a message to the individual soul; but whose function is fulfilled only by being sung in fellowship by the brotherhood who have apprehended the message. And so we must find music fit to express spiritual values in unison.

The essentials of the hymn tune are, first, a simplicity that brings it within a congregation's reach, and, second, the spiritual impression it makes upon them. And, if church song is to rise above a perfunctory performance of an assigned duty, it is equally essential that the music have the quality we call charm,—the gift of approaching the spirit by the avenue of sense, gratified by the appeal of beauty.

The spirituality of the hymn tune is no doubt overstressed in describing it as "an offering to God," which on that account should be solemn and stately, with feeling duly repressed. The music is sufficiently spiritual if it encourages the deeper enterprise of offering ourselves to God. To that end an element of sentimentality is allowable: probably necessary so long as we are human beings rather than academic liturgiologists.

The essential of simplicity can hardly be overstressed. The limits of a congregational tune are so narrowly rigid. It cannot cover the whole hymn anthem-wise, or adapt itself to varying verses as a song may. It must begin and end within the limits of a single verse, to be repeated as often as verses occur. It must be a clear melody that will carry itself without the inner parts, kept within the range of the average voice and the available musical ability.

Great musicians feel the constraint of these limits, just as in hymn writing Tennyson felt the constraint of what he called "commonplace." It used to be pleasant to talk over these matters with Horatio Parker, most scholarly of our composers, who had a part in editing several hymnals and composed some tunes of exceptional brilliancy. He liked to say in private what he is reported as saying publicly, that the hymn tune is quite the lowest form of music. He had no instinctive sympathy with congregational singing, which he found inartistic; and he had an idealist's contempt for the common level and for popularity. One of his earlier tunes, "Garden City," that attained wide vogue, became an offense to him, just as the popularity of John Hay's early ballads became an irritation to that writer. Dr. Parker told me he would recall his tune if he could.

And yet effectiveness need not be a bugbear to an artist. The restraint that adapts a composition to its appointed function is an art motive in itself. The miniature may exhibit qualities as sound as the colossal canvasses of Benjamin West, and is much better adapted to be cherished. Certainly Parker's "Mount Sion" is, within its limits, as good music as his prize opera "Mona." And one can imagine the hymn tune being sung on church occasions till the end of time, while it is doubtful if the profoundly accomplished opera, having had its official hearing, will again be performed.

The moral of which things is that the Church must not submit to an academic decree banishing its hymn tunes from the realm of art, lest the tunes shall be satisfied to clothe themselves in the shabby garments of the outcast, or in the tinsel and motley of the cabaret, as our popular song has already learned to do.

The Church and its pastors must really enlarge their minds to let the hymn tune share whatever concern they feel for the hymns. In the actual administration of hymnody as an ordinance there is no room for distinction between words and music. The hymn and its tune together compose the unit of the hymn as sung, and together stand or fall. An inartistic tune will kill the most poetic hymn ever written. A dull or unwelcome tune will impart to the most spiritual words an atmosphere of insincerity that makes one's spirit shrink. A tune adequate to the spiritual values of the words, interprets them. A great tune does more: it adds something to the printed words by way of suggesting things of the spirit unprinted between the lines.

II. The Primitive Singing

It is a quaint providence that has preserved as a part of our English Bible the names of several tunes to which Psalms were sung, by indicating the title of some familiar song to the melody of which the Psalm was set. Thus Psalm xxii was sung to "A Hind in the Morning"; xlv to "The lilies"; lvi to "The silent Dove of those far off"; lx to "The Lily of Testimony." The ascriptions add nothing to our knowledge of Hebrew music, but they do confer a grace of pedigree upon the hymn tune.[2]

No Hebrew melody survives. The attempt to trace a connection of one or another with traditional synagogue melodies fails because the inherited tunes differ among themselves, reflecting the country and period of their origin. The opinion that the Hebrew music is continued in the ecclesiastical chant of the Roman Church must be relegated to the sphere of pious tradition.

The Hebrew tune had no harmony in our modern sense. It was a unison cantillation, free, and not measured like an Anglican chant, and following more closely the rhythms of the words. The melodies had individuality enough to be remembered and handed down; for there was no way of recording them.

At the Last Supper the company would use the one they associated with the Hallel. Our Lord had no intent of imposing upon His Church His national music or ritual. The particular tune they used did not become an oral tradition, and could not have been made a part of the written gospel, since no system of notation had been invented. I have often thought how happy that circumstance was. If the music had been included in the narrative, as it would be in a modern phonographic record, it would inevitably have acquired a sacrosanct character. It might have formed the basis of a system of church music that would have kept the later Church outside the development of modern culture.

It would be surplusage to recall that our Lord imposed no type of music upon His Church, were it not for the recent order of the Pope (acting as His Vicar) prescribing the sole use in all churches of the Roman obedience of that plain-song music which some claim as primitive. In view also, I might add, of the pronouncements from time to time of Protestant leaders of ecclesiastical music, venturing to lay out its metes and bounds with equal precision but with less authority.

The singing of the Pauline Churches is often made the precedent for congregational song as distinguished from the singing of a later time by officiants. The psalmody most characteristic, the charismatic, was certainly not congregational, but delivered solowise to a listening assembly.

There were practical difficulties in the way of "conjoint singing." There was no common musical standard. It is not clear that Jewish Christians would find the Septuagint Psalms adaptable to the only music they knew. Nor can we say how far either Jew or Gentile brought to the meetings the tradition of simultaneous singing. What was more practicable and presumably more familiar was that simplest type of antiphonal song in which a leader carries the Psalm and the congregation makes such responses as are agreed upon.

Many of the proper tunes of the Psalms had been lost from memory before our Lord's time; and the musical ideals of the scattered Jews must have been already modified by Hellenistic influences. Renan [3] would infer the character of the music not so much from that of the synagogue as from the Eastern practice of to-day. He argues that a common practice among religious communities separated since early times testifies to its great antiquity:

"The chanting with which they accompanied the new hymns was probably that species of sobbing without distinct notes which is still the chant of the Greek Church, of the Marionites, and generally of Eastern Christians. It is not so much a musical modulation as a manner of forcing the voice and of emitting through the nose a sort of groaning, in which all the inflections follow each other rapidly. They perform this singular melopœia standing; the eye fixed, the forehead knitted, the eye-brow contracted, giving an appearance of effort. The word 'Amen,' above all, is uttered in a tremulous voice with bodily shaking."

Instrumental music being still excluded from Greek Church worship, the same method of arguing back from present-day practice, would raise a presumption that the psalmody was unaccompanied.

Calvin at Geneva took a definite stand against it, and ever since "the instrumental music question" has vexed the Puritan conscience. In the days of Puritan ascendancy in England it wrought great iconoclasm. Perhaps it is settled now. But in "cases of conscience" one never knows.

Certainly it is not settled by the record. St. Paul's verb, "psallein," is cited as implying instrumental accompaniment: his "making melody in the heart" is cited as proving that the heart-strings are the instrument referred to. In I Cor. xiv, 7, 8, the Apostle refers familiarly to several musical instruments; but Dr. Porteus, debating *The Organ Question*,[4] detects a note of contempt in his allusion to "sounding brass and tinkling cymbal" in I Cor. xiii, 1.

Perhaps we might agree that the record is noncommital. The enlightened imagination has indeed a great deal to do with the settlement of these questions of history and of conscience. And the Christian imagination continues to hear the blast of Temple trumpets making a loud noise unto Jehovah, and persists in giving audience not only to a voice from heaven as the sound of many waters, but to the voice of harpers harping with their harps as the new song arises to the throne of God itself.

III. Plainsong Melodies

Church music had become little more than recitation when Ambrose introduced at Milan the antiphonal singing by the congregation of his new metrical hymns. For tunes he reverted to the Greek scales or modes; and in four of them composed those Psalm and hymn melodies whose rendering in the basilica so deeply moved the heart of St. Augustine. Readers of his *Confessions* will recall the ecstasy of his delight and the suggestive cross-examination of that delight to discover if his emotions were not sensuous rather than spiritual. And yet the tunes were rudimental, without the charm of harmony, and the voice production distinctly nasal.

On this Greek basis was developed the musical system of plainsong, to which the labors of the great Gregory have attached the name of Gregorian Chant.

To any Christian with the historic sense a worship-music with traditions so venerable makes an *a priori* appeal: to one ecclesiastically-minded there is a heightening in the appeal of the only music the Church can claim as distinctively her own.

When the Oxford Revival turned the English Church mind to Medievalism, a definite movement began, under Thomas Helmore's lead, to engraft the Gregorian music upon English worship. This beginning, in the eighteen fifties, was premature and misinformed.

With the great prominence given to it by the *Motu proprio* of Pius X in 1903, restoring the purity of plainsong and enjoining its use in Roman Catholic churches, a new movement has begun to introduce it into Anglican and Episcopal Churches and some congregations outside. The typical Church of England book, *Hymns ancient and modern*, in its 1904 edition triples the number of plainsong melodies of the original issue of 1861. The newer *English Hymnal* has a hundred; *The New Hymnal* of the American Episcopal Church has fourteen.

Some traces of plainsong influence are in all hymnals: in Lowell Mason's "Hamburg" for instance. Some of its melodies in a popularized form are familiar and useful: "Veni Emmanuel" for instance. With these possibly the plainsong movement might be allowed to rest for the present. It should be cross-examined in the interests of the congregation. The tunes are without the aid of harmony, written in unfamiliar keys, timeless and unbarred. Their beauty depends on adapting the free rhythm to the mutations of the words. They are confessedly difficult even for trained choirs. Badly sung they are totally uninteresting.

Such reports as reach me from Episcopal parishes are uniform in their complaint that the purer plainsong melodies in their *New Hymnal* shut out the people from participating in the hymns set to them. Those who are outside the line of this particular musical tradition may wisely heed a practical estimate by one born in it and long experienced in it. So I quote from the *History and Growth of Church Music* by Father Taunton, a Roman Catholic musician: [5]

"Although I personally admire and take a delight

in joining to the best of my poor abilities in the Plain Chant, yet I am convinced it does not do for our people. It does not appeal to them, it does not awake in them any echoes of the religious life. The impressions it produces are gloom and monotony, and these are not religious. . . . The truth is that Plain Chant is suited to and can only be sung, as it ought to be sung, by the clergy and religious."

Nevertheless the wide concern of *The English Hymnal* with plainsong, suggests that the movement to acclimate it will have to be tried out in the Church of England. Should the movement win through it will no doubt affect the more cultivated congregations in non-liturgical communions, so oddly sensitive as they are to prevailing fashions in liturgical Churches.

I hear already of one pastor whole-heartedly training his people in the love and practice of plainsong. Others of us who cherish no expectation that it will ever be popularized, and are conscious of no wish that it should be, may yet welcome such a training-school. No music teaches so impressively the rightful supremacy of holy words over musical notes. Its measures are the marks of punctuation: its accents the emphasis given to a syllable in careful speech. A training in it would give the habit of unremitting attention to the words of a hymn, so lacking at present. To me it would seem obvious that each melody should be applied only to the specific hymn to which it was so carefully adapted, and that the hymns should be sung in the original Latin, whose speech-values and fluctuating rhythms cannot be reproduced in English.

IV. The Lutheran Chorales [6]

Ambrose's task of finding congregational tunes for new hymns came afresh to Martin Luther. The task was congenial to one who thought the singing of united voices "the most beautiful thing in the world"; and not too difficult for one so familiar with the traditions and so accustomed to the performance of both plainsong and folk song.

Luther invented or shaped the Protestant hymn tune, in that form which, as harmonized and developed in the century following, we are accustomed to call the "Lutheran chorale." Its essence was a sober and elevated but buoyant melody, in the idiom of the songs in which a musical people were accustomed to express their feelings, without any great distinction between those definitely religious or simply human.

Whether Luther composed "Ein' Feste Burg" and other melodies that bear his name is a problem of no great import, as neither he nor his helpers sought originality. Their tunes were largely made up from phrases from plainsong or adaptations of current songs, some of which were already associated with sacred words and some with secular. He was chided for going so far afield as to bring folk songs into the sanctuary. What he did was just what the editors of the recent *English Hymnal* are now so widely commended for doing as a relief from the academic monotony into which Anglican song was falling. And the practical effect of Luther's course was not to secularize church song so much as to turn the current of German music into a religious channel.

Luther's equipment was unique, combining his knowledge of the rich resources, Latin and German, his ability to handle them, his sympathy with plain people, his saving common sense. The twice-told tale of his phenomenal success in making popular song his agent in spreading the gospel and heartening the gospelers does not need to be repeated here.

By a gradual process culminating in the eighteenth century and often attributed to the relaxed spiritual feelings of a cold rationalism, the chorales suffered a decadence like that of plainsong. Their rhythmical movement was often destroyed by reducing them to notes of equal length too much drawn out, which impart a certain dullness in place of the buoyant life and motion of the original.

In this duller form the chorales came into this country and have been presented to American churches: a fact which partly explains why so few have been appropriated. Lutheran worship itself has been a losing struggle to keep to the fore its own hymnody with its proper tunes, during the process of Americanizing successive generations of its people, who acquire a preference for lighter types of song prevailing among the people they daily associate with. There is also a temperamental difference between Germans and Americans that militates against the adoption of the chorales, especially in the slower and heavier form most familiar. Most people respond to this great music sung *en masse* or orchestrated by Bach; but, when asked to join in, some difference in training or something in nervous make-up breeds an impatience in the vocal chords.

Unfortunately there is no pope in Lutheranism to ordain the restoration of the chorale to its primitive beauty. In the meantime a party has arisen with that end in view. It is at least possible that the chorale restored to buoyancy would make a fresh appeal to American congregations. It is indeed worth hoping for.

The extreme Lutheran restorer of the old paths who at times seems to imply that the chorale is the one and only hymn setting for our day, awakens less sympathy. He seems to an outsider to be putting the letter of Luther's tunes in place of the freedom of Luther's method. If any one thing was characteristic of his settlement of Protestant music it was the free spirit that could welcome a contribution of available music from any source whatever, ecclesiastical or human, of a sort that could be adapted to holy words and consecrated by holy associations.

V. The Genevan Melodies

Calvin's problem at Geneva was to find popular melodies that would carry the difficult measures of Marot's Psalms. His attempt to solve it has been treated by a succession of historians as a blot on the record of sacred music.

What Calvin did may be summed up in a sentence. Lacking Luther's equipment he singled out a competent musician, Louis Bourgeois, living at Geneva under needy circumstances, and put into his hands the preparation of suitable melodies. We may be quite sure that he impressed upon the musician just the sort of thing he wanted. Hence the long series of hymn tunes that graced the *Genevan Psalter* of 1551. After Bourgeois had left Geneva, the setting of the balance of the Psalter had to be committed to inferior hands.

When critics protest against Calvin's insistence on unison singing, his repudiation of "curious music," and his banishment of the organ, they are within their rights. Even so one could wish that they might add the historic sense to their critical equipment and, applying to Calvin's musical settlement William James' pragmatic test, acknowledge that "it worked."

Professor Dickinson in his very well-known *Music in the History of the Western Church* is somewhat alone in appreciation of the historical situation. But just what does he mean by calling the Genevan melodies "unemotional unison tunes that satisfied the stern demands of rigid zealots," "not having in themselves any artistic value"? Had Professor Dickinson any first-hand knowledge of this branch of his subject?

Let us turn without further remark to the present Poet Laureate, who has added a grace to our hymnody by his devotion to it, and whose *Yattendon Hymnal* is ample evidence of his musical taste. This is from his twice-printed *Practical Discourse on some principles of Hymn-singing:*[7]

"Bourgeois turned out to be an extraordinary genius in melody." Of his eighty-five tunes in the Genevan Psalter "almost all . . . are of great merit and many of the highest excellence. Bourgeois' tunes are masterpieces, which have remained popular on the continent from the first . . . and the best that can be imagined for solemn congregational singing of the kind which we might expect in England."

It was their beauty that made the Genevan Psalmody and gave it wings. If a hymnologist relied on the French Psalms to prove the power of the hymn to move and sustain the heart, a musician might urge that it was the tunes that won French hearts. He might go further and say that they carried the psalmody across the borders and opened the hearts of many who could not read French. The proof is that it became necessary to translate the Genevan Psalms into most European languages, always preserving the meters and rhythms that so they might be sung to the original melodies.[8]

The Reformed Churches, then, have a musical inheritance of their own; spiritual, artistic. In English-speaking communions it lies practically unclaimed. Among ourselves it has left no traces beyond a reminiscence embodied in the familiar "Autumn" and the survival of the 134th Psalm melody (our "Old Hundredth"), which, like so many chorales, has been reduced to notes of equal length.

The question arises how this loss happened. It was the hearing of the Genevan song that inspired the English exiles of Mary's reign to undertake an English psalm book. Why did they make so little use of what they heard? The answer is quite simple. No one of them could imitate the delicate French lyrical meters which carried the Genevan tunes. They were hard put to get the Psalms into English measures which would pass for verse at all. Their disability finally determined the character of the English Psalm tune as embodied in the *Sternhold and Hopkins Psalter* of 1562; for the most part a rather dull performance; regrettably so because dull tunes are fated to become in time the mother of a dogged congregational hymnody.

Is it worthwhile for English-speaking Reformed communions to claim a musical inheritance so distinctive and so beautiful? Speaking for his own Church of England Dr. Bridges is an enthusiast for the revival of the Genevan melodies, as "thoroughly congenial to our national taste," whereas the failure to bring German chorales into general use testifies to "a difference in the melodic sense of the two nations." The primary difficulty of finding words to fit the French measures Dr. Bridges has begun to meet with some lyrics of his own in his *Yattendon Hymnal*. The editors of *The English Hymnal* have taken up the task, and given currency to sixteen of the melodies. The late Dr. Burnap of Brooklyn was equally anxious to become a pioneer in introducing them into American hymnals. He found the books inhospitable, and the leaders of church music indifferent. It may possibly be that an adequate presentation of the Genevan Psalmody with some simplification of its rhythms might awaken in Reformed Churches something of the pride Lutherans have in their great inheritance. "These tunes," says the Poet Laureate, "in dignity, solemnity, pathos, and melodic solidity leave nothing to be desired."

VI. The English Psalm Tunes

The Psalm tunes of the Reformation period embodied in the English Psalter of 1562 and the Scottish of 1564 are unharmonized, and in their unadorned severity of outline suggest the Puritan influence back of them. They conform to Cranmer's advice to Henry VIII upon translating the liturgy: "The song made thereunto should not be full of notes, but as near as may be for every syllable a note, so that it may be sung distinctly and devoutly."

Some effort was made to provide a proper tune to each Psalm; or, if not, to refer each to the melody of some other. The 8-line C. M. tune was greatly favored. Such Genevan melodies as were used were badly marred in adapting them to English meters, and the new tunes are generally uninteresting. Some half dozen of the 8-line tunes survive in English hymnals, but are less known here.

Either these 8-line tunes taxed peoples' memories or else proved dull, for the harmonized editions of the Psalter that soon began to appear replaced them with "short tunes" of four lines. It is they to which we commonly refer as "the English Psalm Tunes."

William Damon's edition, as early as 1579, gave us "Cambridge" and "Oxford," "Southwell" and (later) "Windsor." Thomas Este's in 1592 gave us "Winchester" and "Cheshire." Thomas Ravenscroft's of 1621 merely reflected the prevailing taste in gathering up from various places a large reënforcement of 4-line tunes. Among his sources was Andro Hart's 1615 edition of the Scottish Psalter, in which a group of twelve appeared as "Common Tunes," applicable to any C. M. Psalm; easier to remember than so many proper tunes. Among them were "Dundee" ("French"), "The Stilt," "Dumferline," "Martyrs" and others that played so great a part in Scottish life, and came to be regarded by many Scottish hearts as having been composed by David himself.

The "short tune" has ever since proved effective, and has often dominated our church song. Nevertheless it marked a decline and not a progress; a lapsing of Reformation fervor, a decadence of the general aptitude for music in Elizabeth's time.

During the long struggle between Puritan and Cavalier the Psalm singing fell between the two stools of high church and low church, and lay in a neglect as great as could befall an ordinance destined to survive. Even the short tunes became unmanageable. With the Puritan ascendancy it fell into a musical collapse, with Parliament wrangling over the version of Psalms to be authorized, and the Scottish Assembly putting forth "Rous' Version" in 1650, mostly in common meter, and (for the first time in Scotland) without any provision of music whatever.

After the Restoration of 1660 something had to be done to revive the lost art of congregational song among a people who did not even know the traditions of a better day. In 1671 John Playford put forth a folio of tunes old and new; complaining in his preface that nearly all the choice tunes were lost and out of use and that very few parish clerks even in London knew enough music to set them. His folio falling flat, six years later he compiled a setting of the old Psalms in a handy twelvemo, with simpler harmonies and a 4-line alternate for every

8-line tune. This became, and for a century continued to be, the musical standard, although contributing very little to our present-day resources.

Outside the Church Dr. Watts regarded his System of Praise as rescue work from the intolerable conditions of psalmody among dissenters. But he depended upon the reviving power of evangelical sentiment, and had no thought musically of any thing more than getting some snap into the few tunes the people knew. It was other hands who found his vigorous hymns an encouragement of a parallel movement to freshen up the musical side also. To this we owe both words and tune of the ringing Easter Hymn, "Jesus Christ is risen to-day." Its appearance was almost simultaneous with that of Watts' *Hymns and Spiritual Songs.*

Within the Church of England the *New Version* of Tate and Brady, at the end of the seventeenth century, had been an effort to better things by providing Psalms more lyrical, singable to current tunes; but its *Supplement* enriched hymnody permanently with three fine tunes of Dr. Croft, "St. Anne," "Hanover" and "St. Matthew's Tune." So far as these were sung at all, even in London, it was disconnectedly, as the clerk droned out the Psalm line by line, and some in the congregation, or some singers representing it, responded with so much of the melody as covered the line.

The average parish church remained unaffected by the *New Version.* It was the deplorable conditions of parochial song that inspired John Wesley to set up the Methodist singing which restored to his people the old fervor of Reformation song. As an educator Wesley taught them how to sing and as an administrator published several tune books. He used German tunes and Psalm tunes, when they pleased him, and, like Luther, secular songs. He was scrupulous both as to musical exactness and spiritual tone. He hated dullness but rebuked "horn-pipes." The "Old Methodist Tunes" are later, and often more florid than he would approve.

Any impression you may get from Green's *Short History of England* that Wesley set all England a-singing Methodist hymns is altogether erroneous. The Wesleyan zeal for song overflowed into the Evangelical side of the Revival through Whitefield and the Countess of Huntingdon's chapels, and even tapped the Church of England through the Evangelical party she inspired. But to the stodgy churchliness of the time the Methodist "enthusiasm" was simply hateful. It was distasteful even to Dr. Watts and dignified dissent. The field-song of the revivals had no more direct influence upon parochial psalmody than the tambourines of the Salvation Army have now upon English cathedrals.

The Wesleyan side contributed little to the common stock of tunes. But a number of our hymns are still associated with tunes used in Lady Huntingdon's chapels or Evangelical services elsewhere. The most striking original contribution is "Miles

Lane," still in England the proper tune to "All hail the power of Jesus' Name."

An abundance of eighteenth century tune books testify in their way to a desire to improve congregational singing. The fresh tunes they offer are an effort to get away from the rigid outline of the old Psalm tune, and may be viewed as presenting a new type.

This eighteenth century hymn tune has two characteristics: its freedom in using two or more notes to a single syllable, often expanding into trills and runs; and its more unconstrained use of vivacious triple time. The Advent tune, "Helmsley," so dear to the heart of Queen Victoria, is an example, perhaps the more delightful for being somewhat questionable.

These eighteenth century tune books must have found their market for the most part among dissenting interests. These more or less florid tunes, associated in our thoughts with the English Church, were as a rule hers only by adoption. William Knapp, it is true, was parish clerk, and made an opportunity to introduce his useful "Wareham" into his Devonshire parish. But Barthélémon's "Morning Hymn" was the peculiar property of a London charity school; Wainwright's ringing melody to "Christians, awake" was an open-air Christmas carol; "Adeste Fideles" was familiar only in Roman Catholic chapels.

The Church of England had a minor part either in

introducing or countenancing the more florid type of hymn tune that marks the eighteenth century development of hymnody. Dr. Burney, writing in 1789, assures us that only two new tunes had been adopted in church services for a hundred years; Dr. Croft's "Hanover" and the "Easter Hymn."

VII. American Song

1. *Psalm Tunes in New England*

The first Protestant tunes heard in this country were the melodies of Calvin's Psalter, sung in Florida by members of Coligny's expeditions of 1562-64, and which became their most lasting memorial. For Le Challeux tells us [9] that long after the break-up of the colony the traveler would catch strains of them uncouthly rendered by the native Indians. But they were of no influence upon American psalmody.

The Pilgrim Fathers brought to Plymouth in 1620 the Psalter Henry Ainsworth prepared in Holland for his English flock. Longfellow has made its name famous, but its music was almost forgotten till Professor Pratt of Hartford analyzed and annotated it. In his *Music of the Pilgrims* [10] he has shown that a majority of the tunes were French, not English, and by public demonstrations has shown how singable they are. The French meters and the long verses became more and more of a hindrance as musical ability weakened under the hard conditions of life. But Plymouth held on to a diminishing remnant of its own tunes till the century's end; when it resorted to the "short tunes" used in the Bay Colony.

For the Puritans had brought to Massachusetts Bay a few copies of Ravenscroft's setting of *Sternhold and Hopkins*, which since 1621 had been the musical standard at home. Endicott's copy is at the Massachusetts Historical Society; and there lately appeared at auction the autographed copy of Judge Sewall, to whose diary we owe our knowledge of the almost unbelievable straits to which New England psalmody was reduced; with the members of the congregation refusing to sing in time, and sometimes to sing the same tune. It took ten years of controversy to persuade the New England conscience that a regulated tune did not infringe upon individual freedom to worship God in one's independent way.

By the time it ended hardly a congregation could even attempt more than three or four of the forty C. M. tunes which a note in *The Bay Psalm Book* of 1640 had pronounced available.

As a first step toward recovery the edition of 1698 printed at the end a group of fifteen tunes; the earliest printing of music in the colonies. Somewhere between 1714 and the twenties the Rev. John Tufts printed the first American tune book; very small because very daring, with thirty-seven tunes in three parts, all English. His venture found favor, and eleven editions were called for.[11] It was followed in 1721 by *The Grounds and Rules of Musick* of Thomas Walter, another clergyman. My copy contains twenty-four tunes, and is apparently complete; but the book was really a primer.

There is no evidence that any Psalm tune or any music of any kind was composed by a native of this country till we come to two Philadelphia contemporaries: Francis Hopkinson (1737-1791) an amateur who was to become a "Signer," and James Lyon (1735-1794), a Princeton graduate who was to become a Presbyterian clergyman. Both composed tunes and published tune books, and one or the other is the first American composer.[12] Hopkinson's book of 1763 was made and printed in Philadelphia for the united parish of Christ Church and St. Peter's. Lyon's, probably made in Princeton, was published in 1761 in Philadelphia as *Urania*, with a dedication to the clergy of all denominations; who responded by calling for several editions. It contained some tunes of his own, but depended mostly upon the eighteenth century English books, some of quite recent date; and it was the most important thing of its kind as yet done in the colonies.

2. *American Hymn Tunes*[13]

From this date, and for a century, ending in the 1870s, a succession of those oblong tune books, once so familiar, followed with a persistency that implies some demand at the time, and involves ample shelving and a patient mind on the part of a modern collector. Are they worth collecting? From a musical standpoint hardly so: from a historical standpoint quite so. They created the phases through which the developing hymnody found expression in the ordinance of Congregational Song; and in the end they came very close to wrecking it.

These books made and now cover the epochs of the American tune, and of hymn singing from the beginnings to the *Gospel Hymns* of the 1870s.

(a) BILLINGS' FUGUEING TUNES came first; with, as he said, "twenty times the power of the old slow tunes; each part straining for mastery and victory." They were introduced in a series of tune books ranging from 1770 to 1794. William Billings was a grotesque figure of a tanner, short in one leg and short of one eye; self-taught as far as taught, with an entertaining gift of self-applause and a touch of genius; a spiritual brother of Lord Timothy Dexter of Newburyport.

By the contrast of their excitements with the traditional dullness his tunes appealed to the rising spirit of revolution in the colonies. The contagion of their swinging melodies and the thrill of their fugueing ventures carried New England off its feet and effected a revolution in church song. His tune "Chester," set to "Let tyrants shake their iron rod," played a part in the Revolutionary War itself.

"Majesty" was his masterpiece, of a jolly stateliness; and I defy any company to sing it, in its original and uncorrected form, without a thrill.

As an offering of church song Billings' work no doubt is grotesque. The permanent lesson it embodies is that if the Church lets its hymnody grow dull from whatever motive or the lack of any, the irrepressible instincts of human nature for life and color will take the matter of enlivening into their own hands, even to the extent of making the hymnody ridiculous.

(b) Lowell Mason's Work. Billings had started the New England singing school, which rapidly developed into an institution. Psalmody became a recreation, and the conduct of it by itinerant "professors" became a profession. These men were the composers of the tunes and compilers of the succession of the tune books, for which their local connections afforded a market. Some were Billings' imitators: most had perforce to keep nearer the ground, where they were hoping evidently to establish a school of American church music. This was the "New Psalmody" of the singing schools, now seeming so uninstructed and dull, or else so eccentric.

It led to a reactionary movement, that became marked very early in the nineteenth century, to reestablish what they called the "Ancient Psalmody," which might mean the earlier or the eighteenth century Psalm tunes and newer work patterned on them.

This uncertain, if not confused situation, in a dark age of music, formed Lowell Mason's background; and gave an opportunity to introduce what may fairly be called his own type of tunes: in the choral style, sober, dignified, melodious, with very simple harmonies, and with undoubtedly a prevailing suggestion of religious feeling.

Mason was a New Englander clerking in Savannah, when in 1822 he succeeded in having his first tune book printed in Boston under the patronage of its Handel and Haydn Society. It was they who brought him home under assurances of employment as musical leader in Boston churches.

By training the young in day-schools, by his writings and a long series of tune books accompanied by choir training in the art of using them, he improved the performance and established the type of American psalmody. A self-made man whose own acquirements were not such as elevated him out of sight of the average ability of the people, he encouraged a sobering of public taste so tactfully that his tunes still remain very much alive, and are our most characteristic contribution to the common stock of tunes having spiritual value.

At the time he completely dominated the situation. I have a series of letters to and fro between him and various editors, whose purport is a desire on his part to claim property in the tunes that make his books saleable, and on theirs an urgent plea for permission to incorporate his tunes in their own books; without which, they say, they hardly venture to go to press.

Mason's tunes seem to us framed in the very interest of a congregation of limited musical acquirements. It is nevertheless true that he and his active co-worker, Thomas Hastings, put an emphasis upon choir training that inevitably tended to a separation of interests between the skillful choir and the uncultivated congregation. "We must not here be understood as opposed to congregational song as such," Hastings found it necessary to protest in his *Musical Taste*.[14] But in his heart he was quite willing that, until the people acquired more of that taste and a greater efficiency, they should listen to the choir.

(c) The Parlor Music Type. This listening attitude was accentuated in the years between 1850 and the Civil War, at the hands of foreign-born musicians who were brought here to take charge of musical interests in some parish or who sought a leadership in church song. They were ignorant of American traditions and more or less bored by Lowell Mason's ascendancy.

The listening attitude became inevitable under the ministrations of Henry W. Greatorex, an Englishman brought here in the late thirties to take charge of the organ at Centre Church, Hartford. His *Collection* of 1851 introduced into an abounding popularity the hymn tune of a daintier type of what may be called parlor music, the sacred quartette rather than choral music. Thus arose the necessity of the quartette choir to do justice to the music and to dominate the hymnody for many years.

We need not share the liturgical abhorrence of the part-song as an expression of church song. At its best it may happen to enrich the family song of the brotherhood. It is enough to say that at the time of introduction it was hopelessly beyond the capacity of American congregations. The practical working of this movement was to restore in our Protestant churches the canon of the Council meeting at Laodicæa in 363 to the effect that "beside the Psalm singers appointed thereto, who mount the ambo and sing out of the book, no others shall sing in church." The choir rendered the hymns from the "book," the oblong tune books they alone had on their ambo, and which were frequently changed in the interest of novelty. The congregation listened, and in many churches turned toward the choir loft to see as well as hear the performers.

Of this collapse of popular song I have collected abundant evidence covering the Congregationalist, Episcopalian, Presbyterian and Lutheran communions: In all of them it became indeed a matter of synodical concern. In all of them the subjugation of the congregation had become complete. Seated between a pulpit asserting its supremacy in everything but song and a choir loft monopolizing the song, the people were no longer a band of common worshipers but merely an audience attending a performance of worship.

(d) The Congregational Tune Book. If the hymnody was to be restored to a Protestant basis the first step was to begin where Luther and Calvin had begun; to provide suitable music and to get it into the hands of the people who were to sing it.

The ground had been prepared to some extent by Joshua Leavitt, a specialist in revivals, in his *The Christian Lyre*, which in 1831 began to appear in monthly installments, with easy tunes set to each hymn or group of hymns. To Mason and Hastings it seemed to undo their work by lowering the musical standard and appropriating undesirable secular melodies. They printed a rival book in 1832, *Spiritual Songs for social worship* on the same plan, but somewhat more sober in tone. It is notable that both books regard "the psalmody of larger and more dignified assemblies" as a thing quite apart.

These 2-part tunes, these little books, are only for families, social gatherings, prayer meetings, revivals. Both became popular, and must have persuaded many Christians that they might do their own singing. Perhaps we may regard Leavitt's book as marking an extension of camp-meeting and Methodist song into other communions, and that of Hastings and Mason as an unintended preparation for a movement that was to put the musical hymnal into the hands of worshiping congregations.

But not for some years. The church hymnal with tunes in our American congregations is due more to Henry Ward Beecher than to any other man; closely followed as he was by the Andover Faculty. He craved the inspiration of congregational singing in his Brooklyn church both as affording an opportunity for expressing feeling and as creating the best atmosphere in which to preach.

He proposed to his organist, Darius E. Jones, the preparation of a small book of hymns and tunes, *Temple Melodies*, whose success inspired the larger venture of the *Plymouth Collection* of 1855. So much of a pioneer was he, and so eccentric his enterprise seemed that he found a publisher with great difficulty. But its success was immediate; and the congregational singing of Plymouth Church became a thing to be imitated. A musical edition of the Andover book followed in 1859, and in 1862 Dr. Charles S. Robinson got his hymnal with tunes into many Presbyterian congregations.

These books fixed the type of the American hymnal on the original Reformation lines, and through them congregational singing was restored. They hardly established a specific type of tune, beyond a preference for what was simple and melodious, with a preponderance of examples of the Lowell Mason order, by that time become a churchly tradition. On this general basis the American church tune remained, until enriched and modified by the influence of the Oxford Revival.

(e) THE TUNES OF THE OXFORD MOVEMENT proved so persuasive in various communions on this side of the water that they may conveniently be dealt with here, as marking a phase in the development of our American hymn singing.

Their novelty lay largely in freshness of melody and delicacy of harmonization. They were foreshadowed to some extent by the work of such men as Samuel S. Wesley, composer of "Aurelia," Henry J. Gauntlett and Sir John Goss, but emerged full stream in *Hymns ancient and modern* of 1861 and its supplement of 1867; the classical hymnal of the Oxford Movement. Its new tunes were largely the work of four men: its editor, William H. Monk, composer of "Eventide"; John B. Dykes (a disciple of Mendelssohn), composer of "Lux Benigna"; Joseph Barnby (a disciple of Gounod), composer of "O Paradise"; and Sir John Stainer, composer of "Blessed Home."

The new melodies were sentimental rather than strenuous, and often plaintive; supported in the inner parts by what may be called a sentimental use of close harmonies, in the manner of current part-song as over against the independently melodious counterpoint of the old Psalm tunes. They express more the feeling of the Oxford Revival than its resolution, the spiritual sentiment of the individual rather than the sense of corporate worship. And therefore they complemented rather than replaced the more churchly type of tune being provided by Helmore, Redhead and others favoring the plain-song tradition.

Such as they were, they at once won the favor of church musicians and the hearts of the people in ever-widening circles, and became the characteristic Victorian hymn tune. They were made familiar in the American Episcopal Church through importations and reprints, and almost as soon in the Presbyterian Church through the *Presbyterian Hymnal* of 1874. Until now they seem in many communions like a part of the common inheritance.

At length their half-century's unbroken popularity is suffering from a reaction at the hands of church musicians so extreme that they are unable to express their disdain in terms of that moderation which alone is convincing.

Mr. Geoffrey Dearmer has a paper in *Music and Letters* for January, 1925, on "The Fall and Rise of the Hymn Tune," in which *Hymns ancient and modern* is represented as "plunging religious music into an abyss" from which only now there is a movement to rescue it. He is following the lines laid out in *Worship and Music* of 1918,[15] by Chancellor George Gardner, with Bishop Gore's approval.

In the course of his argument the Chancellor makes occasion to refer to "the thin and perhaps rowdy way" in which Dykes' tune to "Eternal

Father, strong to save" and Barnby's to "For all the saints who from their labors rest" express their sentiments. Incidentally he refers to "the vulgar lusciousness" or "cheap world-weariness" of other tunes of Dykes, and compares Barnby's tune to "When morning gilds the skies" to the "clank, clank of machinery."

The offense of these tunes lies no doubt in the personal feeling they express. If the protest is valid it ought to go deeper. The real question is whether hymns of personal sentiment are proper for public worship. Granting that they are to be so used, the tune of personal sentiment logically follows. If "Abide with me" is a proper church hymn, Monk's tune is its "proper tune." It would be mere affectation to set it to a plainsong melody. If we are to make a church hymn of "Lead, Kindly Light," Dykes' tune, as the Cardinal himself admitted, is its inevitable setting.

Most of us probably believe in a religion of feeling and a hymnody that expresses it. So perhaps I may be allowed to set down a judgment of these tunes more favorable than that just quoted.

They are beautiful music of their kind, but the kind is mainly part-song. They do not exhilarate our feelings, as some of the old Psalm tunes do. They do not greatly feed our Christian virility, but they bring a message distinctly spiritual. They fit into the spiritual interpretation of life. They have a curious gift of suggesting to the imagination that a yearning after holiness is the way to God's peace.

In respect of the practical effect of these tunes on American worship, after fifty years' experience, it may be enough to quote the estimate of Professor Dickinson in his *Music in the History of the Western Church* to the effect that the value of their influence in inspiring a love for that which is purest and most salutary in worship music has been incalculable.[16]

(f) The Gospel Hymn emerged in the last quarter of the nineteenth century: a new type which for all practical purposes may be called a type of tune, more or less involving the hymn itself. We are indeed told just now by Dr. Lapsley in his *The Songs of Zion* [17] that the development of the English hymn through two centuries and a half "falls into three clearly defined periods: *The Age of Psalmody*, *The Age of the Standard Hymn*, *The Age of the Gospel Hymns*." If these are the three epochs of hymnody, the proper word is not "development" but decadence. Happily they are not.

The Gospel Hymn was merely a modern instance of that lighter popular song that has always hovered at the borders of church worship; a rival or supplement of what Dr. Lapsley calls "the standard hymn." It is the successor, in reality the outgrowth, of the evangelistic or camp-meeting "spiritual" of the early nineteen hundreds, more or less modified by the tripping Sunday school melodies which William B. Bradbury introduced, and further developed in the work of such men as Root, Doane, Lowry, Bliss and others.

Their work was appropriated in Dwight L. Moody's English campaign and his later call upon American churches to add evangelism to worship. Unable to tell one tune from another, Moody selected the Lowry-Bliss type of music because he had observed its emotional appeal to the masses. At the hands of his associate, Mr. Sankey, an untrained singer producing striking elocutionary effects, it combined the functions of song and homily.

The hymns and tunes were embodied in a series of six books ranging from 1876 to 1891, under the title of *Gospel Hymns and Sacred Songs*. Apart from formal church worship these books for a time monopolized the field, partly by the popularity of the songs, partly through the rigid protection of copyright.

The books passed freely into the Sunday school and prayer meeting, and into the church worship of some parishes whose atmosphere was congenial. The extraordinary vogue of the *Gospel Hymns* is within the memory of some of us. Others can get some sense of it by reading Miss Greene's *Cape Cod Folks;* the story of life in a Cape village in the heyday of *Gospel Hymns*, which run like a refrain, almost like a theme, through the story from beginning to end.

The Gospel Hymn continues the form and manner of the old spiritual and is equally charged with emotion. It has a contagious melody, pathetic or ringing, a frequent march or dance rhythm, and that peculiar thinness of effect which comes of continuing the harmony unchanged through the bar. It makes use of solo effects, of repeats, of burdens and climacteric catchwords, with of course a generous use of "that most sociable of musical devices," the chorus. It is, in other words, the conventional type of music appealing to the crowd as distinguished from more thoughtful and cultivated people.

The use of this music by the class of people to whose taste and attainments it fairly corresponds, especially in evangelistic work, was not very generally contested even by musicians to whom it seemed insipid and vulgar. But the proposal to introduce it into church use did suggest the themes of warm debate.[18] Are these emotional songs really spiritual, and are their obvious effects an excitement of the senses or a religious stimulant? Should the efforts of the public school to improve children's taste be thwarted by the Sunday school? Can the Church afford to sanction a standard of worship music below that of the educated society in which it moves?

The debate will still go on no doubt, but the verdict becomes of less importance year by year. The *Gospel Hymns* occupy a far background now. Most are forgotten. Those once popular are staled by repetition. The few that may find a place in church hymnals convey no covert threat of an "era of Gospel Hymns," and may or may not prove an addition to church song of some permanence.

(g) THE LATER DEGENERACY. The more pressing problem is how the Church is to deal with the evangelistic and popular song that has taken the place of the *Gospel Hymns*, appropriating their name and now rivaling their popularity.

From the day of Moody and Sankey, whose aims were undoubtedly spiritual, and whose royalties on the song books were turned into their work, the course of this popular song, as distinguished from the church hymnody, has been an uninterrupted decadence.

Each of the evangelists who followed Moody felt that he too must have his personal song book. He could not reprint the copyrighted *Gospel Hymns*, but must look for writers and composers who could imitate their method and reproduce their reactions. When the new men failed to please the new public, it became necessary to resort to more sensational and vulgar musical effects to arouse an unresponsive audience. And lately it has seemed expedient to the great and profitable trade which has developed in purveying this material, to descend to the level of current popular song, which has never been so decadent as now, and to imitate quite frankly the music of the dance hall and the cabaret, the jingle, the rag-time, the one-step, the uproarious chorus.

I should not have supposed, *a priori*, that within

a sober-minded communion any pastor could be found to countenance, much less to introduce into the church life this fatuous verse, this degenerate music. Unhappily in the only communion of which I have much knowledge at first hand, the hymnal correspondence of its publishing house reveals that some of its pastors are making the venture of laying this strange offering on the altar of the Lord. Their self-justification, one supposes, would be taken from the atmosphere by which their young people are already surrounded in daily life; from the prudence of giving the young all the thrills they are accustomed to in secular songs but freed from the indecencies of which current song are so full. An interesting case of reciprocity in a North Carolina city is reported by Professor Poteat of Wake Forest College.[19] It was a dance at which the orchestra used one of these "sacred song books" to provide music enough for the whole evening.

No good purpose would be served by attempting at the close of these lectures any minute delineation of a situation as unpleasant as it is prevalent in certain sections of the South and West.[20] There is the less occasion for it since Professor Poteat has devoted a whole book to the subject. His *Practical Hymnology* exposes and handles the situation with an aggressive frankness for which he deserves only thanks. It has been suggested that his book would be more effective by being more urbane. Urbanity no doubt is a grace and in debate more effective than invective. But Professor Poteat has lived in close contact with this new song, with full opportunity of studying its reactions in young lives. And the warmth of his protest is perhaps inevitable. There were occasions when even our Lord lost His urbanity; and one can conceive the rendering of some of these present-day songs in His presence as possibly presenting such an occasion.

VIII. The Inheritance and the Outlook

In looking back over the long history of the hymn tune, we discern clearly enough a development as well as a genealogy.

While the Gregorian music prevailed, the hymn tune was nothing more than an adaptation to the words of the hymn of the one type of ecclesiastical chant that covered the psalmody and other prose of the Daily Office. With the Reformation the modern hymn tune began as an effort to apply contemporaneous standards of popular music to sacred song. And on that line it has developed ever since. Each new phase of the hymn tune stands in a living relation to the generation that produced it, and expresses the ideal and idiom of the music popular at the period.

The lesson of it all is that this whole process has neither conserved any special type of tune that is sacrosanct nor developed only one type that is imperative by reason of spiritual fitness. The original

Jewish sacred music did not percolate through the Empire, and is now beyond recovery. The Gregorian Chant was not originally sacred, but appropriated from Greek Pagan music. And both Luther and Calvin embodied the form of the popular song and drew freely from its stores. These older tunes and those that followed have acquired the sacredness of holy association, but they have no traditional authority, as setting up a norm and model or even a type of what is sacred. They suggest rather the wisdom of doing what our fathers did, of adapting our music to the needs of our own generation.

When that is said, the whole body of the historical hymn tunes remains with us as our inheritance, and the best of them are still a part of the available resources of congregational song. Leaving out the lost melodies of Israel there is hardly a type of the historic hymn tune that is not represented in our modern hymnal. The people are not indifferent to them or to so many of them as they can understand, and whose musical idiom comes natural to them. To an instructed and imaginative Christian the historic tunes bring a spiritual glow they only can impart, a sense of the Church's unending song. That is what an Anglo-Catholic gets out of the Gregorian Chant, and what a Scotchman gets out of Dundee.

Some things need to be done before we can fairly estimate our inherited resources. The Gregorian melodies have at last been purified, and are now in the way of being tested in actual use, if indeed the game be worth the candle. The German chorales need to be restored to their original rhythms before we discard them as dull and heavy. The old English Psalm tunes need to be rescued from the undeserved neglect into which they are falling by a retrial in their original form. They are not properly presented in our hymnals, and our organists and people have quite lost the art of handling them. "St. Anne" is a very great tune, but sung in modern speed with a sort of staccato effect, it is not a means of grace.

But we ought not to be asked to revive any of the older tunes merely for the sake of any curious interest they may have rather than for a spiritual message. And we ought not to be asked to carry indefinitely any of the traditional American tunes that, for whatever reason, have ceased to inspire or to please, and have become luggage in the hand rather than melodies in our hearts.

There are also some sources of congregational song that have hardly as yet been tapped.

First of all, the wealth of Welsh tunes which express the most warm-hearted and inspiring congregational song that is now practiced. Owing to the isolation of Wales linguistically and to the nineteenth century contentment with Anglican and Victorian hymnody the English-speaking people until quite lately have given very little attention to Welsh song. Its unapproached fervor and the enthusiastic reports brought home by the delegates to the Presbyterian Alliance at Cardiff in 1925, suggest a thorough study of the Welsh hymnody at its sources. In the meantime Dr. Vaughan Davies in *The English Hymnal* and in his later *Students' Hymnal* has made accessible a large selection of Welsh tunes, some of which invite a testing with American congregations.

The English Hymnal of 1906, just referred to, is the most interesting because the most experimental of modern hymn books, and the first that has threatened the overwhelming supremacy of *Hymns ancient and modern* in the Church of England since 1861. Unfortunately it bears the hall-mark of highly developed Anglo-Catholicism. One of its striking features is its revival of no less than forty-two of the traditional folk song melodies of the English people and their adaptation to church use. A large body of these had been unearthed by the labors of the Folk Song Society, and the ability of their quaint and simple beauty to reach the hearts of English people has again been demonstrated in congregations adopting *The English Hymnal.* Whether the same thing would prove true of our American congregations is by no means assured, but it is one of the things waiting to be tried out. *The English Hymnal* made also a narrow use of the American spirituals which used to figure in our hymnals as "Western melody" and which Dr.

Lorenz likes to think of as our American folk songs. Upon them, at all events, it seems reasonably sure that the "Negro spirituals" now attracting so much attention were based.

The general state of congregational song affords no real ground for discouragement. But, compared to what it has been and what it may be, it is respectable and comely rather than satisfying. There is a great deal of half-hearted and perfunctory singing in our services; an atmosphere of indifference or inattention from which it must be rescued.

It were quite vain to deny that our pastors are to a considerable degree responsible for this. The indifference in the pews is very apt to be the reflection of the indifference in the pulpit. Wherever the extreme liturgical or artistic ideal of worship prevails there develops a disposition to delegate its expression to the choir; especially to the boy-choir, whose only fault is that it is so pleasant to listen to. But the extreme homiletical ideal of worship is quite as detrimental. If a preacher obviously intends to dominate the worship, he is just as obviously encouraging in his people that habit of becoming listeners rather than participants, which so easily develops into a habit of becoming listless, from which it is hard to rouse them.

When the pastor tries to do so by pulpit appeals urging the Christian duty of joining in singing the praises of God, after the fashion set by William Law in his *Serious Call*, he is beginning his belated reform at the wrong end. Surely there are Christian duties enough without adding that of singing to their number. The spirit of song is spontaneous, and outside the sphere of ethics. The condition precedent is not a sense of duty disturbing the conscience, but the word of Christ dwelling richly in the heart that breaks forth spontaneously into songs of thanksgiving and gratitude and fellowship. Its utterance will rise above the sphere of duty and flourish in the atmosphere of spiritual pleasure. "Sing praises unto His Name; for it is pleasant."

And so we get at the two-fold function of the church hymnal; that of deepening the spiritual life out of which song flows, and of lifting Christian hymnody out of the sphere of duty by encouraging the spirit of song.

The immediate need surely is to get the church hymnal back into the hands of the people where Luther and Calvin first put it. At present it is hardly more than a part of the furniture of the pew racks in our churches. As regards hymnody the congregation is very much where it would be in knowledge of Scripture if there were no Bibles except those in the pulpit or the lectern. Very few of the people now have hymnals of their own. They do not read the poetry devotionally; they do not sing the tunes at home or in social gatherings: they have no familiarity with either and consequently little love for them. When the hymn is given out in church they often start to sing without knowing what is coming or whether it expresses their personal feelings in any way; and they can hardly be expected so to sing either in the Spirit or with understanding. For they are continually singing a strange song.

So inspiring and uplifting can the spiritual ministry of poetry and music to human lives be made that I venture to propose this task and opportunity of getting the hymnal back into the homes and hands and hearts of Christian people as one of the most rewarding that can engage us.

Before this can be done we must agree that the hymnal itself shall be made more lovable than it is. In the desire to incorporate the traditional as well as the timely, to gratify a wide range of taste and opinion, and especially to cover every possible occasion and sermon theme, the church hymnal has become cumbersome to the hands in which we would place it, too encylopedic and utilitarian to appeal to the heart.

It is the demand of our pastors, who require all sorts of hymns for all sorts of purposes, and not the judgment of the compilers, that makes our hymnals so big and pads them with so much that is dull. This encyclopedic range may be a pastoral convenience but it is a spiritual blunder. So much material discourages devotion and defeats the memory; and a good deal of it transcends the true sphere of song. It is regrettable that so many pastors prefer the prosaic hymns to those that are lyrical, and, if the reports from the parishes are true, only too often confine their people within a dull and monotonous round of them.

I like to foresee a time when our pastors shall discover that the highest utilitarianism lies in cultivating the spirit of song for its own sake. For the spirit of Christian song is simply the Holy Spirit Himself, making melody in the heart.

NOTES

NOTES

LECTURE I

1. The title of Dean Church's lectures of 1874.
2. On the 148th Psalm.
3. It can be read in Skene's *The Lord's Supper and the Passover Ritual* (a translation of Bickell's *Messe und Pascha*), Edinburgh, 1891, p. 207.
4. *Cf. Encyclopædia Biblica,* art. "Hallel"; and Schürer, *The Jewish People in the time of Jesus Christ* (English trans., Div. ii, vol. i, p. 291). Edinburgh, 1885. The Hallel as a whole covered Psalms 115-118.
5. Skene, *ut supra,* pp. 174, 207.
6. *The Expositor,* '85b, 3.
7. In preface to his (*Cambridge Bible*) Commentary on St. Luke.
8. *The Presbyterian,* Edinburgh, February 1, 1872.
9. *Some Thoughts concerning the present Revival in New England,* Boston, 1742, p. 181.
10. Robert Baxter's *Narrative of Facts characterizing the Supernatural Manifestations* is scarce. The substance of his testimony is in Dean Stanley's *Corinthians* (Ed. 1882, pp. 252 ff.).
11. *Seasonable Thoughts on the State of Religion in New England,* Boston, 1743, p. 126.
12. *A faithful Narrative of the surprising Work of God . . . in Northampton;* 2nd edition, London, 1738, p. 15.
13. John McPherson, *Commentary on Ephesians,* Edinburgh, 1892, p. 390.
14. *The Athenæum,* April 11, April 18, May 30, 1914.
15. *The Odes and Psalms of Solomon,* 2nd edition, Cambridge, 1911, p. 89.
16. *Das apostolische Zeitalter der christlichen Kirche,* 2nd edition, Freiburg, 1892; English trans., London, 1895, vol. ii, p. 259 ff.
17. Walter Lowrie, *The Church and its Organization,* Longmans, Green and Co., 1904, p. 213. Principal Lindsay also follows Weizsächer in his *The Church and its Ministry,* London, 1902, p. 45.

LECTURE II

1. *The Stromata,* book vii, chap. 7.
2. *Ibid,* chap. 8. That new hymns of human composition as well as Psalms are referred to, Clement makes plain by remarking incidentally that "an unworthy opinion of God preserves no piety either in hymns or sermons or writings or dogmas" (chap. 7).

3. *Ad uxorii,* book ii, chap. 8.
4. *De spectaculis,* chap. 29.
5. *De carne Christi,* chap. 17, 20.
6. Socrates, *H. E.,* book vi, chap. 8.
7. Basil, *De Spiritu Sancto,* 73.
8. It appears in the list of works on the back of the Hippolytus-statue.
9. Eusebius, *H. E.,* vii, 24, 4.
10. *Ibid.,* v, 28, 5.
11. *De Spiritu Sancto,* 73.
12. *Amherst Papyri,* part i, No. 2.
13. In his *Heresies,* 67.
14. *Ep.* x, 96.
15. *Apology,* chap. 39.
16. Book ii, chap. 4.
17. *Apol.,* 1, 13.
18. Eusebius, v, 28, 5.
19. 53rd *Homily* on Heretics.
20. Referred to in the Muratorian Fragment.
21. Socrates, *H. E.,* vi, 8.
22. *Gen. Hist. of Christian Religion and Church,* Torrey's trans., ed. 1871, vol. ii, p. 354, n. 3.
23. Mgr. Pierre Batiffol, *History of the Roman Breviary,* rev. English ed., Longmans, 1912, p. 8.
24. Sozomen, *H. E.,* viii, 8, 1-5.
25. *Vide* "Africa and the Beginnings of Christian Latin Literature" in *Am. Jour. of Theology,* Jan. 1907.
26. *Cf.* H. Leclercq, *L'Afrique Chretienne,* Paris, 1904, vol. i, chap. 5, "Les Dialectes."
27. *Ibid.,* appendix.
28. *Comm. in Ep. ad Gal.* ii, pref.
29. Tertullian, *De Jejunio,* chap. 10.
30. *Cf.* Batiffol, *op. cit.,* chap. 1; and Duchesne, *Christian Worship,* English trans., London, 1903, chap. 16.
31. The texts of this and the following rules and canons are conveniently gathered in U. Chevalier, *Poesie liturgique,* Tournai, 1894.
32. For possible exceptions, see Batiffol, p. 140. On this point, and on the monastic concern with hymns, *cf.* W. C. Bishop, *The Mozarabic and Ambrosian Rites,* London, 1924, pp. 56, 62, 65, 67.
33. The hymns of the Roman Breviary are admirably presented in Matthew Britt, *The Hymns of the Breviary and Missal,* Benziger Brothers, 1922.
34. For the Sequence any history of the Mass may be consulted; and, for detailed information, John Mason Neale, *Essays in Liturgiology and Church History,* London, 1863, pp. 359-370; and Julian, *Dictionary of Hymnology,* art. "Sequence."
35. *The German Mass,* 1526.
36. *Formula Missæ,* 1523.
37. *Ibid.*
38. Preface of 1545.

39. Luther's hymns are to be found in innumerable editions; accessibly in James F. Lambert, *Luther's Hymns,* Phila., General Council Publn. House, 1917; with translations, the hymn book prefaces and other interesting matter. The prefaces may also be found in R. Massie, *Martin Luther's Spiritual Songs,* London, 1854. Luther's various liturgical proposals, on which his use of hymns in public worship depends, are translated and annotated in Richard and Painter, *Christian Worship: its principles and forms,* 2nd ed., revised, Philadelphia, [1908]. The Lutheran chorale is discussed in the last of the present lectures.
40. *Formula Missæ.*
41. *Ibid.*
42. Preface of 1525.
43. The letter to Spalatin.
44. Christoffel, *Huldrich Zwingli,* Elberfield, 1857. English trans., Edinburgh, 1858, p. 150, n.
45. *Calvini Opera,* ed. 1863 seq., vol. Xa, 12.
46. "Alterum ut ad publicas orationes psalmorum cantio adhibeatur."
47. The author gave a much more detailed account of the origins of the Reformed Psalmody in a former Stone lecture, printed in *Journal of The Presbyterian Hist. Soc.,* Phila., for March and June, 1909.
48. *Calvini Opera,* vi, 165-172.
49. This phase of the subject is popularly portrayed in Prothero, *The Psalms in Human Life,* var. eds.
50. *Cf.* Quick, *Synodicon,* vol. i, p. xliii.
51. The process of transition from a strict Psalmody to an evangelical hymnody in English-speaking Churches is fully set forth in the author's *The English Hymn,* N. Y. and Phila., 1915.

LECTURE III

1. *Zachariae Ferrerii Vicent. Pont. Gardien. Hymni Novi Ecclesiastici ivxta veram Metri et Latinitatis Normam a Beatiss. Patre Claemente VII. Pont. Max. vt in divinis quisque eis vti possit approbati et novis Lvdovici Vicentini ac Lavtitii Pervsini Characteribus in Lvcem traditi. Sanctvm ac necessarivm Opvs. Breviarivm ecclesiasticvm ab eodem Zach. Pont. longe brevivs et facilivs redditvm, et ab omni errore pvrgatvm propediem exibit.* [colophon:] Impressum hoc diuinum Opus Rome in ædibus Ludouici Vicentini et Lautitii Perusini, non sine Priuilegio.—Kal. Febru. M.D. XXV.

   Mgr. Batiffol (*op. cit.*) discusses Ferreri and the humanist Breviary promised on the title-page in his charming way; and to his translator I am indebted for the English version of the lines quoted.
2. The English Psalter (commonly called *Sternhold and Hopkins,* or the *Old Version*) appeared in its completed form from the press of John Day at London, as *The whole Booke of Psalmes,*

collected into Englysh metre by T. Starnhold, I. Hopkins & others: conferred with the Ebrue, with apt Notes to sing them withal, Faithfully perused and alowed according to thordre appointed in the Quenes maiesties Iniunctions. Very mete to be vsed of all sortes of people priuately for their solace & comfort: laying apart all vngodly Songes and Ballades, which tende only to the norishing of vyce, and corrupting of youth. [Followed by two texts and imprint]. *An.* 1562.

3. *A new Version of the Psalms of David, fitted to the tunes used in churches. By N. Tate and N. Brady.* London, 1696.
4. *The Psalms of David in meeter. Newly translated, and diligently compared with the originall Text, and former translations: More plain, smooth, and agreeable to the Text, than any heretofore. Allowed by the Authority of the Generall Assembly of the Kirk of Scotland, and appointed to be sung in Congregations and Families. Edinburgh, Printed by Evan Tyler, Printer to the King's most Excellent Majesty,* 1650. This came to be familiarly known as "Rous' Version."
5. *The Muse in Council: being essays on Poets and Poetry,* Houghton, Mifflin Company, 1925; pp. 60 ff.
6. George Saintsbury, *A History of English Prosody,* vol. ii, Macmillan, 1908, p. 531.
7. *The English Lyric,* Houghton, Mifflin Co., 1913, p. 6.
8. It is worth while to remember that Arnold's respect for John Ellerton's hymns, his tribute to Watts' "When I survey the wondrous cross" just before the hand of death touched him, are just as real, as sincere, as his personal distaste for "Nearer, my God, to Thee." His criticisms arose out of the conviction that hymns are to be judged as poetry, to be criticized for their violations of poetic canons. So elevated a point of view is inspiring, to say the least of it, and any critical remarks its occupant cares to send down are not disposed of by the fancied discovery of a manner of condescension. They ought to be welcomed.

LECTURE IV

1. "[Ambrose's] hymns were used to convey correct Catholic doctrine to the minds and hearts of his people." Matthew Britt, *op. cit.*, p. 21.
2. This definition, so far as it is true, is itself the echo of a great soul, the late Richard Holt Hutton.
3. In some hymnals the editors think it needful to print the people's part in the responsive Psalter in large capitals, like a child's primer. A prominent pastor writes me of the importance of getting the entire hymn on a single page, even though the left hand page at a given opening, saying that his people close the books as soon as the bottom of a page is reached.
4. *A Collection of Hymns,* New York, 1831.
5. One who questions this may revert to Dr. Alexander's preface of 1831: "The systematic method of arranging hymns accord-

ing to their subjects, as commonly pursued, is incapable of being rendered perfect or even satisfactory; for it often happens, that in the same hymn there is such a diversity, as to the nature of the emotions and sentiments expressed, that it cannot with propriety be referred to any one head." Dr. Alexander proceeds to arrange his 742 hymns alphabetically according to the opening word—an arrangement that appeals to the eye readily until we reach those beginning with "Oh."

6. Anna Robeson Burr, *Religious Confessions and Confessants,* Houghton, Mifflin Co., 1914.
7. Since the date of these lectures I have endeavored to embody this mission of good cheer in a hymnal, *Christian Song,* New York and Philadelphia, 1926.
8. Clarence Edward Macartney, *Reconciliation through Jesus Christ,* Office of the Gen. Assembly, Presbyterian Church in the U. S. A. [1925], p. 9.

LECTURE V

1. *Hymns and Choirs: the matter and the manner of the Service of Song,* Andover, 1860.
2. Boston, 1857.
3. P. 202 ff. "The Old School Collection" was the *Psalms and Hymns* of 1843.
4. London, 1787. Often reprinted and widely used here.
5. See my "American Revisions of Watts' Psalms" in *Journal of the Presbyterian Historical Society,* Philadelphia, for June and September, 1903, and separately.
6. *A Selection of Psalms and Hymns for public and private use, adapted to the Church of England,* Sheffield, 1819.
7. *Memorials: part i,* Roundell Palmer, Earl of Selborne, Macmillan, 1896, vol. ii, p. 464.
8. *Memoirs,* by Holland and Everett, London, 1855, vol. iv, p. 70.
9. Preface to *Hymns for the Christian Church and Home,* 1840, p. xi.
10. All these things I have since attempted in *Christian Song* already referred to.

LECTURE VI

1. The general course of the development of Church Music may be followed in Edward Dickinson, *Music in the History of the Western Church,* New York, Charles Scribner's Sons, 1902. Edmund S. Lorenz, *Church Music: What a Minister should know about it,* F. H. Revell Co. [1923], aims to meet the needs of Seminary classes in Church Music. The best account of the history of Psalm and hymn singing in England is the introduction to *Hymns ancient and modern: historical edition,* (in folio), London, 1909. See also Grove's *Dictionary of Music,* art. Psalmody. James T. Lightwood, *Hymn Tunes and their Story,* London [1905]; and J. Spencer Curwen, *Studies in Worship Music,* 1st and 2nd series, London, n.d.,

are interesting and dependable. Books such as Brown and Butterworth, *The Story of Hymns and Tunes,* Am. Tract. Soc., New York [n.d.] should be avoided or used with greatest care.

2. John E. Peters, *The Psalms as Liturgies,* Macmillan, 1922, p. 49, puts the meaning of these titles to the question.
3. *Les Apôtres,* Paris, 1866, pp. 99 f.
4. *The Organ Question. Statements by Dr. Ritchie and Dr. Porteus, for and against the use of the Organ in Public Worship in the proceedings of the Presbytery of Glasgow,* 1807-8, Edinburgh, 1856, p. 96.
5. Ethelred L. Taunton, *The History and Growth of Church Music,* London, Burns and Oates, n.d., pp. 107 f.
6. Archibald W. Wilson, *The Chorales: their origin and influence,* The Faith Press, London, 1920, is a recent and useful study of them.
7. In *The Journal of Theological Studies* for October, 1899, and separately by R. H. Blackwell, Oxford, 1901.
8. There is a bibliography in F. Bovet, *Histoire du Psautier des Eglises Réformées,* Neuchâtel, 1872; continued in O. Douen, *Clément Marot et le Psautier Huguenot,* Paris, 1878-9. The last named is the fullest presentation of the Genevan melodies and the subsequent harmonizations of them.
9. Charles W. Baird, *History of the Huguenot Emigration to America,* New York [1885], vol. i, pp. 37, 68.
10. The *Music of the Pilgrims: a description of the Psalm-book brought to Plymouth in* 1620, Boston, Oliver Ditson Co. [1921].
11. *An Introduction to the Singing of Psalm-tunes, in a plain easy method. With a collection of tunes in three parts.* The date of original publication is uncertain. My copy is a fifth edition of 1726.
12. See O. G. Sonneck, *Francis Hopkinson and James Lyon,* Washington, D.C., 1905; which contains an analysis of *Urania.* For the earlier music of the immigrant mystics, Johannes Kelpius and Conrad Beissel in connection with the Wissahickon and Ephrata communities, see *Church Music and Musical Life in Pennsylvania in the Eighteenth Century,* Philadelphia: Penna. Soc. of Colonial Dames, 1926, etc.; and Julius F. Sachse, *The Music of the Ephrata Cloister,* Lancaster, 1903.
13. Waldo S. Pratt, in *American Supplement to Grove's Dictionary of Music and Musicians,* has given special attention to the tune writers and tune books in his trustworthy way. Frank J. Metcalf, *American Psalmody or Titles of books containing tunes printed in America from* 1721 *to* 1820, New York, Chas. F. Heartman, 1917, supersedes James Warrington, *Short Titles of books relating to the History and Practice of Psalmody in the U. S.,* Philadelphia, 1898. Metcalf's *American Writers and Compilers of sacred Music,* The Abingdon Press [1925], is valuable both for biography and bibliography.
14. *Dissertation on Musical Taste,* Albany, 1822; rev. and enlarged ed., N. Y., 1853. During his prolonged campaign for better church music, Hastings published numerous books and

review articles, as well as tune books; and the memory of a useful man should not be overshadowed by the greater fame of Lowell Mason. But he will live as the composer of "Toplady."

15. *Worship and Music: suggestions for Clergy and Choirmasters,* by George Gardner, M.A., Mus. Bac., London, S.P.C.K., 1918.
16. P. 384.
17. *The Songs of Zion: a brief study of our Hymns,* by R. A. Lapsley, D.D., Presb. Com. of Publication, Richmond, Va. [1925].
18. Those who favor the use of these songs in worship will find the points of Dr. David R. Breed's objections to them in his *The History and Use of Hymns and Hymn-tunes,* Revell, 1903. Those who oppose their use may encounter a warm advocate of the employment of the better of them in almost any one of Dr. Lorenz's books on Church Music. And the whole matter is sanely and impartially presented in Waldo S. Pratt, *Musical Ministries in the Church,* Revell, 1901.
19. Herbert McNeill Poteat, *Practical Hymnology,* Boston [1921], p. 69, n.
20. "Thousands of our churches and Sunday schools are using the *same sort of music exactly* as is jingled forth by electric piano at the picture house, the pony ballet in the theater, and the jazz orchestra in the public dance hall." Poteat, p. 69.

INDEX